THE DRIVE HME

The Youth Athlete/Parent Dynamic
(through our lens as Junior Golf parents)

Featuring advice from prominent coaches, PGA Tour parents, PGA professionals, business leaders, confidence coaches, and professional and college athletes

Mark and Britt McKinney

This book is dedicated to Bobby, Butch, J-Mac and Cole Baby all of whom we look forward to seeing again one day. We are thankful we have such an amazing team of guardian angels and heavenly caddies.

Contents

Foreword

I am excited for this book, not only for the subject, but because of the authors. I love the McKinney family and have had the privilege of working with Ben, the authors' son. I often say children are the way they are for a reason. The reason for Ben being such a coachable, polite, lovable young man isn't hard to figure out.

My job as a Mental Game Coach is to work with athletes on the mental game. In doing so I've seen the impact parents can have. Some seem like the perfect role models. Some are the reason their child needs to see me, but realistically most parents are somewhere in between the two. Trying to figure out how to help your child is difficult. Navigating the complexity of not only the ever-changing sports scenery, but the developing brains of their children isn't a science. It's more of a trial and error.

Mark (who also wrote *Faith on a Sticky Note*) and Britt have not only created an amazing resource for parents, but they have done so in an entertaining and informative way. They are vulnerable in sharing what has worked as well as what hasn't, and they aren't shy in admitting the mistakes they have made.

The McKinneys' reason for writing this book is to take their experiences and use them to hopefully help you on your journey. I'm a stickler for knowing our "why"... our reason. Why do we do something? What is the bigger picture? The importance of knowing that can't be expressed enough.

As you read this book, think about your "why". Why are you in the role you are in as it pertains to your child's athletic journey? Keep that "why" in front of you. Say it first thing in the morning to yourself in the mirror. Say it before attending your child's competition. It will help you evolve and get through the uncertainty. When we know our "why", the how becomes easier. Too often we sacrifice our "why" for short term results.

This book is filled with great advice! A must read for parents of junior athletes. Enjoy the ever-changing journey!

Tami Matheny
Mental Game and Confidence Coach
Author of *The Confident Athlete* and *This is Good*
Founder of Refuse2LoseCoaching

Preface

The Why and How of This Book

We are excited to share this book—this resource—with all who are fortunate and blessed enough to call themselves golf parents. Ben, our now 17-year-old son, was nine years old when he began playing competitive golf. We use the word competitive, but at nine years old—while he was keeping score, shooting his own yardages, and pulling his own clubs—it was more about learning the ins and outs and the dos and don'ts of playing with others, the etiquette of golf, being held accountable to the rules, and adding scores correctly.

We really had no idea the world we were stepping into when we became golf parents -- similar stories emerge, no doubt, from those who are soccer, baseball, football, basketball, lacrosse ... you name it ... parents. The ideas, stories, lessons learned, and resources presented herein are to a large degree applicable in each of those instances, and we invite you to apply the concepts as you deem appropriate to your sport of choice. However, after playing team sports for so many years and then settling in on golf as a focus sport, we quickly learned how truly player controlled the game of golf is. Your player, your child, is on an island once you tell them 'good luck' at the first tee until you hug them on the 18th green. They are on their own -- to deal with the highs and lows, good and bad decisions, and lucky and unlucky bounces. There is no teammate there to save a bad pass from going out of bounds -- or jump on the ball that is fumbled. That realization is both freeing and frightening as a parent -- because if you take off your 'I want to do all I can to help my child succeed' and 'I can help remove those obstacles being faced right now' or 'I want to 'fix' it and make it better' hat -- you will see your child, your player is growing up right before your eyes. Adversity is an amazing teacher if we get out of the way and let it happen.

As parents we failed at dealing with adversity for so many years ... many, many years. Honestly, we still do sometimes. We spent so many hours on a golf course at the height of anxiety when a ball would go out of bounds or in the water -- worried when we saw Ben hit his ball into a bad lie -- devastated when we saw a putt drop for double bogey -- and counting up where he stood and what the likely tally would be at the end of the day. We know we missed a lot of forest for the trees because we spent so much time trying to 'fix' it ... and then one day we looked up and where this boy used to be who had tears in his eyes when things were going poorly stood this young man who acted differently, walked differently, and dealt differently with adversity. And we realized it, like the flipping of a light switch -- it takes the experience of adversity to build a young golfer, a young athlete, into who they are capable of being. It takes shooting 87 in 100-degree weather and being so mad after missing a putt that the next 5 holes are spent sulking only to look back and realize the focus was off and it cost 5 or 6 more shots. It takes hitting three in a row out of bounds at one of the biggest tournaments you've played in and then having to pull it together on the next shot. It takes missing the cut by a stroke at a qualifier for a tournament you've wanted to play in forever to prepare you for the next qualifier you play in.

We will be the first to say this book is not the 'Hey, we solved the riddle and have a player who never gets angry, never gets disappointed, always shoots par or under, is at the top of the leaderboard in everything he plays' -- this is not that at all. What we are saying is -- we have battle scars as golf parents and as a player, many of which were self-inflicted and completely unnecessary because we didn't know what we didn't know. Looking back, we missed so much of the experience for worrying about the outcome and would give anything to go back with the knowledge we have now -- and we hope we can share that with you so you CAN enjoy the experience. We equate it to taking a flight from point A to B ... and in the middle you encounter turbulence -- some mild and some that takes your stomach. Many of us will spend the entire flight staring out the window trying to anticipate the next bump, the next lightning strike or drop of the plane. Then there's 'that lady' -- headphones in, watching a movie and eating her snack as if nothing is going on around her -- as if we are not in a metal tube flying 600 mph through a thunderstorm and bouncing like a stone. And then it hits you ... there is a 99.9999% chance this plane is going to get safely from A to B -- so why in the world would we worry about the bumps in between? And that lady, the one with the headphones in who is enjoying the ride -- that is who we long to be, and that is what this book is meant to do for us all as golf parents -- **to help us focus not on the turbulence, but the journey as a whole.** Knowing when we land, we are going to be in a whole new place ... and that place is fun to see unfold.

A word about the How of this book now that we have given some background on the Why. It has been said that 'Men are from Mars, Women are from Venus' (John Gray even wrote a book about it) -- and when it comes to golf parenting, it is spot on. You will find that mom and dad 'see' the situations differently, sometimes vastly so. We found out pretty quickly the things Mark may be worried about -- 'Is Ben's driver flex right?' 'Did that lesson we just took make a difference?' 'Are his hips going too fast?' -- vary widely from the things Britt was worried about 'I wonder if he's thirsty and needs a drink', 'I wonder if the fact the kid he is playing with who is jabbering away is a distraction', 'I wonder if he finished his math homework', 'He looks mad … I wonder if he's mad.' 'Is he going to be able to bounce back mentally from the missed putt?' - and so on. Which leads us to the How of this book … We agreed early on to operate as a team and stay in our respective lanes -- embracing the Mars and Venus thing, and we think this is a critical component of the advice we will share in this book. As such, for every concept we present -- we will give you the Mark Said and the Britt Said, the 'he said she said', -- the dad point of view and the mom point of view. Mind you, these are not competing views, more so, complementary (although sometimes, Mars and Venus have ended up taking a healthy distance of separation on the course while one realized how wrong the other was, or vice-versa). We also recognize many times there is a single parent shouldering the load all alone -- whether that be mom or dad, and in those cases our hope is you can see and identify with a little of each viewpoint.

As you read, imagine we are all sitting around on the porch outside the clubhouse having a conversation over a glass of sweet tea after a round - and to get the full experience, imagine a full complement of southern accents speaking from the pages.

Acknowledgments

We would not have made it this far without the village of people that we have surrounded ourselves with and who shaped, influenced and co-wrote this book with their love, listening ears, shoulders to lean on and sometimes smacks back into reality. This is a book filled with the collective wisdom of our entire golfing village, and we wouldn't trade them for the world. Our village includes fellow golf team parents, coaches, mentors, golf parents and players we have met in our travels, equipment fitters, and instructors - all too many to name without the risk of omission. You all know who you are, and we love each one of you.

Introduction

What will I Get from This Book?

It is critically important to put it out there right up front this book is <u>NOT</u> the Earl Woods 'How to Create the Best Player in the World' type of thing. We are not saying at all this will help your player shave 10 shots off their game. We have been fortunate in that Ben, our son, has continued to improve and get better - but also keep in mind he may never shoot near par again, he may go shoot 100 tomorrow, and he may decide next week he no longer has the fire and passion to play golf competitively - and that's his decision. His game improvements have come through his hard work and effort and leveraging the team of people he has around him. This book is more so aimed at **how to be the best golf parents we can be, you can be** - which we think does translate into the player getting better - but there is also no guarantee. Golf tournaments have a way of physically and mentally draining to the point of sheer exhaustion … not to mention the toll it takes on the actual kid/player (ba dum, tss).

Hopefully, what you will get from this book is the understanding of not sweating the small things, knowing what to expect, how to handle the bad days, the HORRIFIC days and the great days ... they will all come. Learning how to best support your athlete … the things to say and when to say them, what not to say … and when a silent hug is the absolute best medicine. Who to hang out with at a tournament, who to politely avoid - how to deal with the 'other' golf parents (and sometimes realizing, you are the 'other golf parents') - how nicknames for both parents and kids never go away and how important they are when recalling stories - how important it is for the kids to handle their business amongst themselves - how cruel and kind the rules can be at the same time - learn who's watching you and who you should be watching and why 'stand up straight and smile' aren't just reserved for cotillion - learn when to go up, when to stay behind and why it's always important to be looking - learn why it's so heart-warming to see a kid who may not break 100 smiling when he makes a 40 footer for par - learn why it's important to know kids are kids and they deal with 'stuff' we have no idea about and sometimes that's why they are a little reserved or quiet when normally they are the talker of the group - learn the way you parent doesn't always line up with the way they parent, and it's not our job to raise theirs … it's our job to raise ours - learn to say I'm sorry and mean it and when to lean on someone else to do the talking, not you - that sometimes the pride is just so much that it fills your throat and you cannot get the words out and that sometimes hurt for your child has the same effect - learn the excitement of seeing the relationships that are created and the bonds that will last forever and why those R'ships > C'ships - and learn why this game is so, so hard … and that just when you think they have it mastered, the script changes and the movie is totally different.

This journey can be one of amazing bonding opportunities – or it can be one that risks damaging family relationships (no, really, pay attention to the article we share later about Sean O'Hair). That line can be thin and a slippery slope if the journey is approached with mismatched goals, unrealistic expectations, and a mom or dad who 'wants it' more than the player does. **That line can create some awkward drives home, and our hope is this book can help you avoid more of those than you need to endure.** Golf is an amazing game that will teach us so much about life, adversity, overcoming, failing and succeeding, hurting and healing, winning and losing with grace – and we are all better off if we let it happen organically and enjoy the moments along the way. Looking back, we laugh now about how keyed up we got about things that didn't and don't matter … we were at risk of being those lawnmower parents we swore we'd never be. Luckily, we have an amazing village to lean on who helped us along the way and now have a better perspective, in hindsight, that we hope can be a help to everyone reading this book.

We are particularly proud of and excited about the collection of powerful advice provided in this book by a talented and well-respected group of coaches, athletes, business leaders, and mentors. We have been humbled by the number of people who agreed to offer their guidance in such a heartfelt and genuine way and count it a blessing the new relationships we have been able to forge as part of this process. That section is sort of like the prize in the Cracker Jack box (if you are a Seinfeld fan, 'it's Gold, Jerry - Gold!'), and we hope you can wait until the end to check it out, but we won't talk about you if you sneak a peek early. In addition, we share a wealth of resources at the end of this book in the form of books, Facebook groups and self-written strategies *(you'll soon know what 3PL stands for and as non-scientific as it is, we think it's something that can help)* that we think can be of value to anyone who is holding this book.

You wouldn't go climb Everest without first getting your ducks in a row, nor should you enter into the world of a golf parent with any less preparation. Come see what we learned - laugh, cry, say 'what?', find out what the Cracker Barrel has to do with the book's title, and be amazed right along with us - you'll be glad you did.

Junior Golf Parenting 101

'There is no greater leadership challenge than parenting. When we think about great leaders, we search for sports, politics, business, and fashion.

Visible areas where individuals excel and can touch many who know just a fraction of their lives. It's attractive, rewarding, fuels the leader's ego and bank account.

On the other hand, it's tough to be the leader of someone who knows every detail of our lives. We can't fake it; we have to show up every day in our best shape to gain our kid's confidence.

Every interaction counts, and every day it's a new beginning no matter how well we performed yesterday.'

–JIM ROHN, AUTHOR AND ENTREPRENEUR

Summing up the Journey

Britt said: People often ask me 'if you could go back in time and give yourself advice at any point, when would that be?' For me, I think this would be one of those times, and I would take myself this book and say 'read it, you are gonna need it!' When thinking about the journey as a whole, it reminds me of a description of a scene from the movie *Parenthood* and author Jackie Joens sums it up like this:

> In the movie, *Parenthood*, there is a scene where Steve Martin's and Mary Steenburgen's characters are discussing the difficulties and challenges of parenthood and life. Martin is frustrated and expressing his desire for some control and guarantees in life. Steenburgen states, "Life is messy." Martin replies, "I hate messy!" It is just about at this moment that

Steenburgen's grandmother (who is apparently suffering from some form of dementia) enters the room and shares a story.

Grandma explains, "You know, when I was young, Grandpa took me on a roller coaster. Up and down, up, down. Oh, what a ride. I always wanted to go again. It was just interesting to me that a ride could make me so frightened ... so scared, so sick, so excited ... and so thrilled all together. Some didn't like it. They went on the merry-go-round. That just goes around. Nothing. I like the roller coaster. You get more out of it."

And for us, the roller coaster was something we knew little about when we started ... We had an idea but could have never dreamed of the ups and downs, highs and lows, laughs and tears that came with it.

Several years ago, I was invited to go to Carowinds with a few girls and their children. I don't love roller coasters, and I swore years back at Six Flags over Georgia I would never get on one again. I also have FOMO - fear of missing out - so I just jumped right in the car to join on the trip. I should have known better than to get on a ride without researching it, but as I walked with a little girl in elementary school and two other moms who were eager to get on the ride ... I hopped right on without a fear in the world. I didn't think the ride would be that bad because they didn't look worried or eager at all. When we got ready to take off, they informed me of all the twists, turns, and drops we would encounter. They laughed until they cried (at me) while I held on for dear life. Again, I swore I would never get on another ride again. It was fun, but I thought my heart was going to jump out of my chest.

I get the same feeling each and every time we step onto the golf course.

I swear I'm not going to let the day get to me. I want to be included with all the other parents, so I continue to go and experience the emotional roller coaster on the good days, the bad days, and the okay days. There is no doubt a ride or walk around the golf course can bring up feelings from the pit of the stomach. Some days I laugh until I cry on the golf course at things other parents are doing, but some days it's me who probably should have just stood back and held the bags while everyone else rode the ride.

I've often said I wish life could be run with a remote control. It would

> *What Parents that* **want their Children to Struggle** *do:*
>
> **Demand that their game be "perfect"**
>
> **React angrily or disappointedly in the stands when he/she makes a mistake**
>
> **Make comments like "How could you do that?" after a seemingly simple error. Or, even better, "WHY would you do that?"**
>
> **Focus your comments to him/her on what is true (such as "that was a bad throw") instead of on whether or not your comment will be helpful.**
>
> *–Tami Matheny*

be great to fast forward through those days that are extremely hard, and some days I'd like to rewind and do things over. Those days we would like to pause and soak in the goodness of the day are the best.

But I'm realistic and know we are not given the opportunity to live life like this. In a perfect world we would get on those rides and enjoy them … even the twists and turns … and we would soak in every moment with our children. If I have learned anything, it's that time flies when you are watching your child compete. It seems in the blink of an eye our little boy who once held plastic clubs was celebrating with his teammates and wearing a state championship medal around his neck. I'm so glad I get to be part of it, but I wish I had chosen joy instead of worry most of the days in his younger years.

Mark said: To Britt's point above, I think it would be amazing to track down Marty McFly and take the DeLorean back several years and tell those two naive, wide eyed, wanting-nothing-but-the-best for our son-parents all of the things contained in this book. I think it's probably like that with all of life, though, right? If I had known then what I know now is a common refrain that gets repeated more the older we get and it is certainly not exclusive to the life of parents of athletes. But I do believe if we read about the experience of others, and if we ask questions of those who have done it before we will be much better prepared, less stressed, and enjoy the ride more. With that being said, when Ben first got into competitive golf, Britt and I were living in Georgia and didn't know a lot of people involved in the smaller junior tours in the area (and don't read too much into that - by 'tour' I mean 'collection of smaller people learning to play the game of golf with a set schedule, rules and participants'). As such, we winged a lot of it - a LOT of it. From the logistics to equipment, I spent a lot of time on Google searching for 'youth golf clubs', 'how to prepare for a youth golf tournament', etc. And I got it wrong … more times than not. I found so many articles saying not to cut down adult clubs for youth because the physical specifications were just not conducive to success - so what did I do? I cut down a set of adult golf clubs for Ben to play with - I went against the grain because I knew they weren't talking about 'my son', surely he was different. Not so much - I think I did more to hinder him than help in those early years by letting my pride and the ever-present man-response 'I got this - I don't need to ask anyone' cloud my vision.

I say that to say this - If your child has an interest in the sport of golf - go talk with the folks who know - not the big box stores, either. Go talk to your local golf pro or the hole in the wall golf shop in your area (just ask and you will find out where 'the spot' is) and simply ask - what is your advice on getting my kid started in the game? You will save yourself a lot of headache, I guarantee it.

Once they do start playing - let it be fun and make sure it STAYS fun. Golf is frustrating, and the sooner we begin putting expectations on kids it begins to take the pure joy out of it. 'How do you know that?' you ask - well, I am the same guy that just wrote the previous paragraph. I found myself skewing towards the expectation side ... chasing numbers and along the way it may have felt more like work than fun for Ben. Don't get me wrong, we would have some awesome outings where we challenged each other, and I still remember the first legitimate par he ever made on a Par 3, Feb 10, 2012 - his eighth birthday. Luckily, I got a picture - and if I could bottle up the joy he had in his eyes and his heart that day, I could sell it for a mint. And that is the point I am trying to convey here - if you can find a way to harness their curiosity and continue to celebrate those moments of fun without messing it up with expectations - you will be ahead of the game.

Remember they are not 'as many years old' as we are - meaning, we cannot expect them to react to situations, pressures, obstacles, and opportunities like we would - we have the benefit of experience on our side. As Hernan Chousa, former professional tennis player, author and public speaker, points out, *"We want our kid to perform their sport and other activities according to our knowledge and set of skills. But we have to realize they have their own pace and act accordingly. They need to experience failure to evolve and grow."* This, in itself, may be the greatest piece of advice to be shared in this book so pay attention to it. Coach Dabo Swinney shared that when he talks with his players he will ask them 'have you ever been 30 years old?', and when they share they have not he responds with 'Well, I have'. Same concept, right? We have all this experience but there is no spout for us to pour it into them. We can advise them, share our stories with them … but many things in life just have to be lived and learned, just like we did when we were that age. So, experience their golfing through that lens … it will help put things into so much perspective, and when you see the light bulbs going off as they learn lesson after lesson … you'll know it was all worth it.

Lastly, and we will get into this in more detail later - pay attention to your words, how you say it, when you say it, and why you say it. *"...our words have a significant impact on them (kids). They add or subtract, and they are never neutral."*, says Chousa. Let that sink in - it is sobering. Remember they are indeed kids and that you love them with all of your heart - you will never forget that you do - make sure they never forget either.

When They Decide They Want to Compete

'Golf is about how well you accept, respond to, and score with your misses much more so than it is a game of your perfect shots.'

– DR. BOB ROTELLA

Mark said: I hear it a lot as we are in and around tournament golf - dads asking other dads, moms asking other moms - 'how did you know that little Johnny/Little Sally wanted to get serious about golf and how did you all know when he/she was ready?' It gets said in a lot of ways, but my thought on it is very similar to when you know that the person you have been dating is the one … when you know, you just know. And you don't try to figure out the how just yet. Heck, if someone had asked Britt and me when we got engaged 'how will you support yourselves, where will you buy a house, how will you pay for school, how are you going to manage the different schedules together' we may have just turned and run. Similar, I think, with golf - if we try to figure everything out before we let our kids take the leap then we may never encourage or support them to do it.

What we will talk about here is what begins to happen AFTER you have introduced your kid(s) to the game, they have shown they have an interest in it - they have banged countless balls on the driving range - they have had the opportunity to go experience playing on a real golf course and watched the ball make it from tee box to the ever satisfying made putt. This is the point when a kid has shown interest that 'you know when you know' they want to continue to get better and ultimately compete.

I recommend (again, I am NOT sports psychologist Dr. Bob Rotella here - more so, this is the 'what would I tell myself' self-talking) doing these key things once your child knows they want to compete and get better:

Find a golf instructor they click with and someone who is in it to see them have fun and get better - Ask people in your circle, post the question on Facebook, ask your local pro, and meet with the prospective instructors to make sure there is a personality fit. Instructors range from ~$50 per hour up to as much as you want to spend - in the beginning, lean towards the lower end of the cost spectrum and ensure a focus on the basics. Good golf instruction will be about more than the swing - it will incorporate the 'how to play' aspects, course management discussions, etc - but most of all, it will have a focus on making sure the player gets better WHILE enjoying it and having fun. We had an instructor say we will know he is doing his job well if we get to the point we no longer need to call him - his success is measured by how well he works himself OUT of a job - think about that … his philosophy being the player should learn and own their swing and eventually be able to self-diagnose.

This little nugget will save you hundreds if not thousands of dollars - You don't need every little swing gadget that comes out (there Britt, I said it). Leave that to the instructor, and if they recommend a particular tool, then absolutely go get it. I could open up and inventory the shelves of a small golf store now with the swing aids and such that maybe got used once or twice.

Put them in the right equipment for their age, size and strength - An important piece of getting them started is making sure they have the right tools for the job - namely clubs. There are so many options out there now for junior starter sets so check with your local pro or that same hole in the wall golf shop and get guidance on the best starter set. You will come to find that the length, shaft flex and weight of the clubs begin to matter a great deal as they get older and more accomplished. As they are just getting started, most of the junior sets that the aforementioned folks will recommend are just fine (as I mentioned in the introduction, I got this so wrong so many times … and we survived it all, so if you go into it with half the foresight I did, you will be just fine).

Keeping up with the golf equipment game, though, is not for the faint of heart - kids grow, they get stronger, and as they do - the clubs they need to play their best change. I will give you my best advice by telling you a story. As Ben hit 13 years old, we got him a set of Ping Thrive clubs - a great set that came highly recommended through the channels I mentioned above. I thought to myself as a dad 'you are one smart cookie, you finally have him in the right equipment.' Fast forward to when he got a little older and his swing continued to improve … we noticed as he was playing that what looked like good passes at the ball would go both left and right … he was hitting it everywhere. So, we worked with his instructor to try and figure out the reason, and nothing was apparent - the swing was solid. At this same time, Ben was slated to play in our high school region tournament and went for a practice round. While pulling his clubs out of the back of the vehicle to go to the range to warm up, the shaft of his driver snapped - a total freak accident that ended up being a Godsend. (I will spare you the details of not being able to get his driver re-shafted in time, so we played the tournament with a loaner … be thankful for good friends with nice clubs!).

Knowing we needed a new driver or at least a new shaft, we ended up at our local hole in the wall - which, by the way, is the vena cava of anything and everything golf in the upstate of SC - if you need it and want to trust who you get it from, Bypass Golf in Spartanburg is the place. Super, super people there and one of the Trackman gurus, Wes Reeves, told Ben that before we bought anything new, he should just hop on Trackman and take a look at numbers. We did, and Wes was able to identify the swing flex and weight Ben needed for a new driver. In conversation, we told Wes about the issues we had been seeing with Ben's irons - army golf, one left, one right … and so on. Wes asked Ben to hit a few 7 irons on Trackman and within minutes said 'hey bud, you are WAY over-flexing these things - there is no way you will ever be able to score consistently with them'. What we discovered, by accident, is that Ben's swing speed had picked up a lot since we had first bought those irons and they were no longer a fit for him - we had been playing tournaments and such, wondering why he hit it all over the map - and we had a big piece of the puzzle. We had all endured a lot of head scratching all because we had sent him with a knife to a gunfight, so to speak. (Aside: getting in the right clubs does not automatically translate into you shooting under par each time - it does, though, eliminate variables that can have an adverse effect. Sort of like someone bending your sights on your rifle before you go hunting … if you don't know it, you may end up hitting something every now and again … but mostly by luck).

Invest the time and money to go hop on Trackman periodically so you will know beyond the shadow of a doubt what equipment is needed (same thing - ask your local golf pro, your instructor or at your local golf shop). I think about it like this - I have wondered for years now why my shoulder kept hurting but always figured it was me getting older. I finally got an MRI and lo and behold, there are some tears in there … Trackman is the MRI for a golf swing and equipment - if you want to know in a hurry why it starts left and goes left, it'll show you - take advantage of it! (Bonus Tip: Trackman can tell you if your putter is fit properly as well … lie/loft/length - find the right setup and it's like handing eyeglasses to a man with bad eyesight.)

Get them engaged in a local junior golf series/tour/organization - Ask your local golf pro or if you do not have one, do a Google search of Junior Golf programs in the area. Your state should have a program with local chapters (i.e., We live in the Upstate of SC and within the South Carolina Junior Golf Association (SCJGA) there is a Greenville Chapter, Spartanburg Chapter, Pickens chapter and many more around us and across the state). In addition, you will find other local junior tours and First Tee locations that are focused on growing the game, helping kids learn and compete at all levels - for instance, here in the Upstate, we have been blessed with the folks at the GSA Golf tour who have been wonderful. An incredible organization that we came across as part of our research for this book is Operation 36 Golf (Operation36.golf) which you will hear more about a little later - with programs specifically designed for beginner golfers are offered at over 600 locations in over 15 countries around the world. Long story short, there will be a wealth of organizations to get involved with - talk with them, learn about their mission and how they operate - they are there to support kids and grow the game and are eager to talk with parents and answer questions. (Tip: Check out https://youthoncourse.org/ to learn how juniors can play $5 rounds)

Once you know they have an interest - go ahead and get them engaged in one of the groups outlined above and turn them loose to experience it, explore it, and learn from it. I will share it in more detail in the **Know the Why and Stick to It** chapter about when we first 'turned Ben loose' under the guidance of Coach Mike Carlisle and his junior tour and how frightening and anxious those moments were - not for him, but for us as parents. Main point here is that we missed a lot of the joy of watching him do his own thing for fear that we hadn't done all we were supposed to do to prepare him. What we didn't know is that all of that mattered very little - getting started in and being part of the process was the important step. It's sort of like people that say, 'if you wait until you are ready to have a baby, you never will'. If you wait until they are ready to get them involved in competitive golf, you never will.

Keep up with their need for equipment changes - As a follow up to the Trackman story, I recommend staying in touch with your child's growth and increase in strength and such. Golf clubs have different shaft flexes that correspond to swing speeds (strength/size), and it is super easy to get an idea of where they are and if/when a change may be needed. Don't worry, things don't change overnight, but as you find yourself looking up at a kid you used to look down at - think about getting a check-up. When you notice they seem to be a bit stronger than they used to be when you have the obligatory wrestling matches in the living room -- yeah, go check it out.

Practice doesn't make perfect, it makes permanent - The instructor can help guide this one but pay attention to it. It is most fun to spend practice time banging balls away with a driver and neglecting the 100 yards and in wedges, the chipping and the putting. A good breakdown I have heard shared many times is 70/30 short-mid game to full swing or 'big swing' as we call it. So whatever the practice time is - break it into those percentages (+/-, not an exact science). The kicker being that in every round all golfers are going to hit one off line from time to time and have to punch out. Getting up and down? My money is on the 70/30 guy. Our local golf pro loves a focus on shots from 100 yards and in and devoting a lot of practice to them in that 70%.

Keep a finger on the pulse to make sure they are still enjoying it - This entire book is really an expansion of this topic, to a degree, but check in with your player often and make sure they are still enjoying it. And, if they say 'this isn't for me', respect that and support their decision.

If they think they want to play college golf: Go ahead and get a copy of Looking for a FULL RIDE by Coach Renee Lopez and join the Facebook group by the same name. Coach Lopez is a 14-year coaching veteran at all levels including D1, D2, D3 and NAIA as well as serving as NCAA Compliance Director. Coach Lopez offers her advice to both parents and junior athletes in the **Advice from People Who Know**. One of the best nuggets she shares, in my opinion, is to ensure that the college you choose passes the 'Broken Leg Test' ... if your athlete went to that school and suffered a broken leg and could not play their sport - would they still be happy about the environment, the location and the educational opportunities? We have close friends that have shared their saga of wasted years because their daughter went to a school that was golf focused versus aligned to her desired field of study ... and she ended up behind two years in course credits as a result. Their advice - **'focus on the education piece first and let athletics come second'**.

Britt said:

Let your motherly instincts take over - As mothers we know (most of the time) what our children are feeling or the mood they are in. I remember when Ben was little, and he was learning to walk and would fall, or he would bump into something ... I would quickly look at him and tell him to think about something else. I knew his first reaction to falling or bumping his head would be to cry. I tried to teach him to think about something else. When, not if, he has a bad hole on the course I always try to refocus his mind on something else. It might be by offering a snack or drink, pointing out something unusual on the course, or asking him a question about a random topic. Most of the time I ask him what he wants to eat after the round or what his plans are for tomorrow. It's all a strategy. As a mother we want our children to focus on the good things in life. If the round is going down the tubes, I try to do everything I can to make him realize life is about more than just those four hours on the course. I'm sure a coach would argue I need to let him refocus on his shots, but sometimes in life we need a fresh restart having nothing to do with what we are upset about. Most tournaments do not allow speaking to the player during the round, so make sure when you do offer drinks, snacks, etc that your comments are loud enough so that everyone can hear and knows you are not trying to provide advice/coaching.

Manners Matter - As golfers, the kids get to experience some amazing locations and super nice courses (they will also play their fair share of 'goat tracks' as Mark calls them). Manners do matter, and I can tell you from experience that making sure your player tucks his shirt in, takes his hat off while inside, and treats the property and people with respect goes a LONG way.

Invest in good walking shoes - I learned this tip late in the process. I should have been a boy scout because I like to be prepared. After the first few tournaments, I began to take everything to the course but the kitchen sink. I had a cooler full of all kinds of drinks, a basket with every kind of snack you can imagine, and a backpack that could run triage in a war zone. This past year we were in a tournament where spectator carts weren't allowed. I had separation anxiety from all my goodies, but I also saw we could survive without all those extras. We were going to be okay! Within just a few weeks I realized my tennis shoes would need to be upgraded, but I also realized walking released some of my anxiety because I was constantly moving. By walking and following Ben play golf, I wasn't driving ahead and sitting with anxiety and pressure in my chest waiting for him to hit. It was therapeutic for me to walk and a blessing in disguise. I suggest always walking to help with your own nerves and feelings of unrest.

Have high expectations about schoolwork - In all honesty, most of the people who read this book, the McKinneys included, aren't going to have a professional athlete on their hands. Realistically, we have to prepare for the worst (in this case it really isn't the worst... our child will need an education and a job to survive life) and hope for the best (our child will have the benefits of a professional athlete's salary). I remind Ben daily that school is important and an education can't be taken away from you. I can't argue that many people make it in life without a formal education but having a degree in an area is just a little bit of insurance in cases when you need a little help in life. Ben lives in the house with a father who doesn't use his degree of study in his job and a mother who wouldn't be where she is without hers. He has seen the benefits of both. I want him to always have that option, and I know in our house my role is to make sure he has done his homework, studied for tests, and completed assignments. It isn't easy. It's frustrating and often ends in eye rolling and teeth sucking! No matter how late we get home from a tournament or how long he practices, he knows his schoolwork has to be done.

Playing for Pixie Sticks and Oreos probably isn't a good idea - In Ben's younger years, I would always joke around with him and his group about playing for Pixie Sticks and Oreos. It worked when he was younger, but as he grew and began to take the game more seriously, I learned it would usually result in him crashing pretty soon after having the sugar high. Eating something sweet always makes me feel better for the moment, so naturally I thought it would be the same for Ben. Recently, we learned to stay away from the sugar and have planned snacks for him to eat at scheduled times. In fact, I'd like to add it usually isn't a good idea to play for anything. Ben has walked down the fairway asking for a dog, new shoes, a club, and anything else a teenage boy can think of wanting. I often just give him the motherly look and let him know his wishes aren't going to come true. I'd like to think one day he will look back and say he played because he enjoyed it!

Always tell them you love them. It's human nature to pick out the bad things we see in a round but focusing on a few good shots and saying 'I love you' can make a bad day a little better. The player may think about those bad shots over and over, but redirecting his/her thinking to how proud you are and how much you love him/her can help. There is always something good in a round. You find it and share it.

When to Call in the Troops

'Life's battles don't always go to the stronger or faster man. Sooner or later the man who WINS is the man who THINKS HE CAN.'

– VINCE LOMBARDI

Mark said: One of the hardest things for a dad to do is admit we don't know how to do something - 'rewire the house to make the lights twinkle? Oh yeah, I got that' - not! The more Ben played, the more I found myself having to admit I did not have all the answers to questions he was asking me, and we found ourselves in situations where I needed to phone a friend. I have already shared the importance of getting a good golf instructor for the player to work with, which for me, took care of a lot of questions. (I watched and listened to a lot of lessons because secretly, I was trying to apply it all to my game - didn't translate.)

As Ben got older and played more and more, the one particular area I found myself failing to help him was around the mental side of the game. I would watch Ben, who had all the tools, get derailed by a bad hole and end up in a funk. When things were good, they were good … but when adversity hit … it would hit hard and was tough to overcome. When he got into pressure situations, we could watch as everything sped up for him ... and he struggled. I had heard one of my fellow golf dads on our team mention before his son had worked with a lady named Tami, and she was a mental coach. I'll admit, my first reaction was 'don't you have to be a little crazy to have to work with a sports psychologist?'. Even when I asked this dad about it … I recall myself whispering - even when no one else was around, because it had this 'feel' about it. I was assured it was nothing like that at all, and after placing my first call to Tami Matheny I realized I had just met one of the most important resources we could have - for both player and parent. Upon further research, I began to see this Mental Game and Confidence coaching is as real as rain - and it is so

> "That's the difference when it comes to the final round. A player standing on the first tee knowing versus a player standing on the first tee hoping."
>
> *–Karen Stupples, former LPGA and LET player, Golf Channel Analyst*

powerful. Sessions are confidential and Tami works with athletes to provide techniques to use to manage adversity, stress, and approach games and matches with confidence. We never ask what they talk about, and Ben is free to share with her anything and everything he has on his mind. As a side note, our high school golf team won the state championship in May 2021, and Tami got to take a photo with 4 team members she works with. I'd like to think she is just as proud of her boys as we are, and I know she was a piece of the puzzle the team needed to be successful.

What's interesting is how many times I have given Tami's information out at golf tournaments since we started talking with her. I will hear parents say 'Johnny/Sally is having so much trouble overcoming adversity … they just get angry and can't recover - I wish there was something we could do to help'. It's so interesting that this part of the sport - any sport - that is so critical to kids learning to battle adversity and overcome challenges - cannot be solved through better technique or running more sprints. Between the ears lies a critical space … and I am so happy we tapped into resources that can help. I provide the information for Tami's resources at the end of this book and believe me when I tell you, mental/confidence coaches are just as powerful for the parents as they are for the athletes.

> **"Success in golf depends less on strength of the body than upon strength of the mind."**
>
> *–Arnold Palmer*

Britt said: I thought 'my child is perfect and surely doesn't need any mental help'. I'm not going to lie here, when Mark suggested we let

Ben see a mental/confidence coach I thought he was the one who needed mental health (he could probably use a little help too, though). My heart hurt to think my child couldn't handle life without help from someone else. I remember the course I was at, the porch I was on, and the moment I saw the mental coach approach Ben at a local golf course. Another mother came over and said, 'That's Tami, the mental coach! WHO is she here for?' My heart sank because I knew she was about to go sit inside with my child. I had no choice but to answer. I shyly said, 'She and Ben are meeting to discuss some things to help him during his rounds.'

She immediately smiled and wanted to know the cost and if I thought she would see her child. It was then I realized it wasn't a bad thing. I have been reassured time and time again of how good his sessions have been because I have seen a difference in his actions and attitude. It's one of those things where I wish I had my remote control to see how easy and much better life could be if I wouldn't let what others think about me worry me.

I should have known all along it would be fine for Ben to talk to someone else because as a teacher I have taught students who wouldn't listen to parents but would do anything for me. Sometimes children need other adults to reassure them instead of their parents. Children still don't believe in us parents 100%. The added tips and strategies a child learns from a mental/confidence coach are lifelong skills and not a quick fix for a short period of time.

What Matters, What Doesn't

Mark said: We have a member of our high school golf team whose favorite saying is 'it don't matter, dude'. No matter what the situation, pouring down rain, winds gusting, 100 degrees, club breaks, a putt lips out - whatever it is, you can count on this young man to say 'it don't matter, dude'. For all the grammar police getting uneasy right now, he is well aware this isn't' quite correct - but I can tell you if you try to say 'doesn't' .. it just loses its juice!

> '5 by 5 rule: If it's not gonna matter in 5 years, don't spend more than 5 minutes being upset about it.'
>
> –*Anonymous*

In fact, he's said it so much that every member of our golf team parent crew now finishes our sentences with the phrase when we know we are talking about something we cannot do anything about that in reality, really does not matter ... dude. What I as a parent have come to realize and appreciate is that what does matter is the effort, the attitude, and the commitment of playing with a joy and appreciation for the game - and in those instances of team competition, that you are playing for the greater good and something bigger than just yourself. What I have come to appreciate in the grand scheme of things does not matter is whether on a given day Ben shoots 74 versus 78. Or, 69 versus 79. This is a hard one to really embrace and commit to - but in the end, it doesn't really matter 'dude'. If you let yourself, you can get lost in the 'oh man, we just made a bogey ... which means the best we can shoot is 75 ... and how will that look on a golf resume?', you can get lost in defining your child by the number they shoot versus the person they are and are becoming. I know this because I have been guilty of this very thing.

What does matter, dude? It matters that we have raised (are raising) a young man with a big heart, who is respectful of others, who has a love for this game and his teammates, who has learned and is learning to deal with all sorts of adversity and come out on the other side a better person. It matters when he tees it up on a given day that he does HIS best, not MY best, or his mother's best and sometimes those numbers are great and sometimes they are ones to be forgotten. We are excited for you to get to the **Advice from People Who Know** section of this book as there are so many nuggets there that help with defining what does and does not matter.

Britt said: It took several years, but I have come to the realization I am replaceable at work. As often as we sit on a high horse and think 'no one else can do my job', we also have to realize what is important in life. When I was asked to move to an administrator position (I work in education), I requested not to work the normal 240 days a year. I knew I wanted the opportunity to watch my children grow up as teenagers and spend time with them before they left our home. I never dreamed those extra days off would be spent walking around a golf course following Ben. People often joke and say I have a break during the summer and don't work every day, but they don't realize the work it is to follow Ben. I wholeheartedly believe a mother's job is first to be a mother and then a worker. He might argue that some days I need to step away from him on the course after he has been met by my gritting teeth, but I know one day he will look back and remember I supported him.

Every family and every situation is different - many families are not able to be there as often as others, heck, there are times when our schedules don't let us make it to tournaments, and we have to enlist Katie Britt, our daughter, or other parents to help out. Don't think that I think bad of those parents who can't come and watch their children or the parents who have been told by their children they can't come watch - I respect those decisions and I completely understand. Being there is a sacrifice of time, money, and other opportunities you could be participating in. We laugh now when people ask, 'where are you going on vacation?' and we get to share that we don't really take a full vacation, they are sort of split up into little trips here and there in 1-3 day chunks (that we wouldn't trade for anything in the world).

There are so many good things about being on the course watching your child on the good and bad days. In all honesty, I missed the moment Ben won his first golf tournament because of work. I survived, he survived, and I'm hopeful he won't look back and say he remembers I wasn't there

> **Your job will forget you ever worked there. Your child will never forget that you weren't there.**

(although I did get to watch it on Facetime!). After experiencing a plethora of emotional days on the course, I think it is really important to be there on the bad days more so than the good ones. As a mama, I want to be there to support him and help him when he is hurting. I also need to make sure he acts like he has some sense when the day goes downhill. In all honesty, go with what you think. You will know if you are needed or not on the course with them, and it's always helpful to make friends amongst the group so that you can have someone to fill in for you if you can't make it.

Mark said (again): After Britt wrote the above about the importance of 'being there' it made me think about my childhood and playing sports. I never remember a time when I looked into the stands or the sideline and did not see my parents there. From scrimmages to state championship games, they were always there and looking back now that I am a parent, I realize the sacrifices they must have had to make. When I became a father, I set a personal goal if I could be there, I would be there. For me, as a long-time traveler for business, that meant taking some wonky plane routes to get home in time - some 3 AM wake up calls to fly out the day of a meeting rather than the night before. Like Britt above, I am not trying to make myself out to be some super dad - because I am far from it - there are stories within our circle of dads and moms who have flown all night from overseas and made it back just in time for a tee time. My point is this, we get one lap around on this globe, and I want to soak up as much time as I can watching my kids grow into the people they are becoming. So when it comes to what matters and what doesn't, I think this is a key one - be there if you can (and if they want you to be). I had the opportunity to spend time in Denmark a few years back and it was during a time Ben and his teammates were finishing their middle school basketball season - I still have the screenshots on my phone from the Facetimes we did (God love Britt for holding the phone up that long) so that I could watch the games from 4,300 miles away and 8 hours ahead). Be there. If you can. It matters, (dude).

On Watching Them Fail

A man found the cocoon of a butterfly. One day a small opening appeared. He sat and watched the butterfly for several hours as it struggled to force its body through that little hole. Then it seemed to stop making any progress. It appeared as if it had gotten as far as it could and could go no further. So the man decided to help the butterfly. He took a pair of scissors and snipped off the remaining bit of the cocoon.

The butterfly then emerged easily. But it had a swollen body and small shriveled wings. The man continued to watch the butterfly because he expected that, at any moment, the wings would enlarge and expand to be able to support the body, which would contract in time. Neither happened! In fact, the butterfly spent the rest of its life crawling around with a swollen body and shriveled wings. It never was able to fly.

What the man in his kindness and haste did not understand was that the restricting cocoon and the struggle required for the butterfly to get through the tiny opening were nature's way of forcing fluid from the body of the butterfly into its wings so that it would be ready for flight once it achieved its freedom from the cocoon.

Sometimes struggles are exactly what we need in our life. If we were allowed to go through our life without any obstacles, it would cripple us. We would not be as strong as we could have been.

THE BUTTERFLY - AUTHOR UNKNOWN

Mark said: I am going to come at this topic from two different angles that will hopefully end up in the same spot. First, I want to talk about the concept of failure and how sometimes … we aren't failing, we just have the wrong expectations. And secondly, I will talk about how critically important failing really is (in golf and in life).

I have heard for so many years that golf was about managing misses and not so much about the good shots. I 'heard', but never really 'listened' to it until I got the opportunity to watch a LOT of junior tournament golf. I think I had fallen into the trap of watching a lot of professional golf on television and seemingly always seeing the good or great shots. But the more I watched players play ... the more I realized, you do, in fact, miss more than you hit it exactly where you are looking. You see, "perfect is the enemy of good" - Voltaire.

Ben and I had several discussions about what it meant to succeed or fail on the golf course. Looking back, I wish we had spent a lot more time here before we really embarked on the journey. So many times we would go out and play together, and I would watch him get frustrated if he came up short, or went a little long, or missed it left of the green or the fairway, or missed a putt. It took a while for me to figure it out, for us to figure it out, but he was measuring himself against perfection on every shot (just watch your player and others ... so many measure themselves against perfection and it creates a 100% opportunity to feel like a failure.) No one can be perfect on the golf course, it is just not possible - so if you go into a round expecting perfection, you are going to 'fail' quickly - and once we 'fail' it can start a snowball of lost confidence and lack of focus on subsequent shots.

As we dug into this, Ben and I spent a lot of time talking through what he considered a success and what he considered a failure. For instance, we talked about tee shots and what the overall goal was - 'is the goal to hit it exactly where you are looking OR is it to advance it to a position where you have the opportunity to have a clear shot to the green?'. Now, don't get me wrong, there is tremendous power in aiming small and having specific targets - to the point that the story goes that Ben Hogan once asked his caddy for an aiming point on a blind tee shot and his caddy advised him 'that group of trees' to which Hogan replied, 'which limb?'. Aim small, miss small is the idea here ... but my bigger point being ... if you don't hit 'that limb', don't go throwing a fit - evaluate if you achieved the overall goal of putting yourself in a position to accomplish the next goal - getting on the green. It's very similar to what Dabo Swinney says about punt returns and how he coaches his guys - first, catch the ball, second, retain possession of the ball and third ... do something with it. Sounds simple enough - but it applies to golf as well.

When we started looking at playing golf with this new outlook, it really changed the perspective. That, and the fact that when you look at the PGA tour statistics - it really puts your 'desire for perfection' into a whole new light. Based on PGA Tour averages, pros hit just about 65% of fairways and 66% of greens (better players more, average players, less - but you get the picture). So, if the pros are missing ⅓ of everything they aim at and they are the best in the world, how can we expect more of ourselves?

I think Phil Mickelson summed it best when he was heard on camera after an errant tee shot sharing something to this effect (not exact quote, but this is the gist) - 'it doesn't have to be good, just safe' - meaning that he didn't care where it landed as long as he was able to swing at it again.

Ben's high school golf coach shared the following blog post from Coach Jeanne Sutherland with our team at a pre-season event, and it puts the idea of perfection into a nice perspective. Coach Sutherland joined the Nebraska Women's golf team in 2021 as Associate Head Coach and prior to that was Head Coach at both Texas A&M (1992-2007) and SMU (2011-2021). The post is shared below with expressed permission from Coach Sutherland, and she also offers powerful insights in the upcoming **Advice from People Who Know** section.

IS PERFECT HOLDING YOU BACK?

https://12monthsofgolfinvail.blogspot.com/2018/03
March 26, 2018, Coach Jeanne Sutherland

After 25 years of coaching, I often get asked what I see as differences in today's youth. I generally reply that they've changed little over the years. However, one thing I see is young players today believe in the fallacy of perfection and use that as a measure for all that they do. It is a far more prevalent mindset than I saw in my early days of coaching. In those days, I would have an occasional perfectionist and my goal would be to find something for that player to perfect which was in her control. Now, most juniors coming up claim to be perfectionists and I would agree with their assessments.

If you have an approach of perfection, you will rise to the top of the game when you are young. You will work hard, you will hone your skills, you will accept nothing but the best and your scores will beat the kids who are just playing the game to play the game. However, there will come a day when that approach won't work for you anymore. Perfectionists plateau at a level below greatness, because they can't accept their mistakes and move on. The reliance on perfection can be changed and these players can learn to control the controllables and move on, but it takes determination. It takes letting go of the habits of their thoughts and replacing them with different habits that embrace patience, acceptance and accountability.

The first step is to stop focusing on what isn't happening. That might sound easy, but that seems to be the biggest roadblock to letting go of perfection. If you are a young player and you shoot 69, do you come in and lament the two six footers you missed? If you make a 95 on a test, do you get upset that you didn't make 100%? If you hit the first four greens and have tap ins for par, are you upset that you didn't make any birdies? If you make two long par putts, do you wonder why you can't do the same for birdie? These are thought processes of perfectionists. Nothing is good enough. Patience isn't embraced. Progress isn't recognized. The brain gets caught up in thoughts of the past. Comparisons against a perfect self are constant. The goal of perfectionists on the golf course isn't one of scoring, but one of proving themselves to themselves at each step.

Sadly, we as coaches, parents, teachers and society in general support this way of thinking. Our questions aren't about mindset, patience, learning, positive self-talk or decision making. Instead, they are about results, mistakes and problems. This reinforces the idea of focusing on what isn't happening instead of what is. The focus is aimed at problems instead of solutions. Go back to the last paragraph and look at the ways perfectionism gets in the way. How can you change it? After any score or any day, look at your stats and pick one or two skills that can be better. Golf will always present room for improvement. If you are doing things right, make sure you celebrate them and remember to include them in your game plan going forward. This process should happen after every round and stay consistent.

If you make a 95, celebrate the A and learn what held you back from 100 to better understand it. Go talk to the teacher and see how your thinking differs from hers. If someone congratulates you on your score, thank them. Don't tell the story of the stupid mistake you made that cost you that other 5%. Don't tell them how you SHOULD have made 100%. You probably beat them on the test and by not accepting their compliment, you are ostracizing yourself and being self-centered.

If you have four tap-ins for par on the first four holes, make sure your self-talk is focused on staying patient, applauding your good play that offered you opportunities and understand you are on the right track. If you make two long putts for par, celebrate them and feel the momentum they bring your game! With every step you take on the golf course, you can relax, enjoy the nature and your playing partners or you can grind over what didn't happen on past holes. In a conversation this weekend, one of my players admitted to me that being a perfectionist is exhausting. I would agree. I see it sucking the joy out of the game and in the bigger picture, out of life.

> "Anyone can see the adversity in a difficult situation, but it takes a stronger person to see the opportunity."
>
> –Drew Brees

Your goal in golf is to get the ball in the hole. If you chunk it on a par 3 and it hits a rock on the edge of the water and bounces close to the hole, do you celebrate or focus on how you hit it? How you answer this question will tell you all you need to know about yourself. After all my years of coaching, I've learned that the players who laugh and relax and accept an easy two understand *the game. The players who put the club away and act as though they need to do better are playing a different game that has nothing to do with golf. They are playing against some perfect version of their own skills. It seems as though our culture of focusing on process supports this reaction instead of celebrating the good result of a bad swing. The constant talk of process has led many young players to be less accountable for their scoring. While we all know that being in the moment and doing things right to prepare for a shot is important, it isn't more important than the end result of the shot. Accountability can't be for process alone, nor can skills be separated from outcome. Golf is a bottom-line game and that line is the score. By focusing on the imperfection of individual skills and not on the score, you both protect your ego from bad results and fail to build confidence based on your ability to overcome those imperfections.*

The last thing I'd suggest if you are a perfectionist is, think of your game as your craft. It is what you do, not who you are. You love your craft and want to be good at it. You want it to produce wonderful things, the same as an artist produces beautiful art. Then, identify yourself as a craftsman. It is a life-long journey based on production of good scores. You add skills to your craft and build your game and understanding of it to fit any course and any condition. How you identify yourself and your journey is very important and will allow your mindset to be one of patience, skill building, learning and continually based on solutions. You will learn to become accountable for your overall scoring or what you produce instead of each individual swing you make during your round. Good luck and I know you can change this mindset and become a GREAT player!

Even more eye opening when we were headlong into measuring ourselves against perfection was the data we read in *Every Shot Counts*, by Columbia Business School professor and father of the **Strokes Gained** statistic Mark Broadie which compiled Shotlink data of over 4 million putts on the PGA tour - the best putters in the world on the best surfaces in the world.

I would watch as Ben and his buddies would get frustrated when they missed a putt from 20 ft, 30 ft, 18 ft, 10 ft. And I think the table of data that follows provided more sanity than anything else we ever came across … it showed us the indisputable percentages from different distances. *As a teaser of how powerful the statistics are, how many putts over 21 feet does a PGA Tour golfer sink in a four-round tournament? Five? Seven?* ***The average is only 1.5.*** Main lesson here 'why would you beat yourself up for missing a 20-footer when the best players in the world on the best surfaces on the planet only MAKE that putt 15% of the time?'. It once again gave more meat to the discussion of 'what is our goal here?' - if we have a 30-foot putt, what is our REAL goal based on the numbers? The goal is to two-putt, and if it falls in, that's a bonus, and it relieves us from having to throw our hands up or slap our leg when it runs by the edge. After it's over, did we two putt? If so, yes, we accomplished our goal. If not, we take a look at why and learn from it. Stop chasing perfection … and it changes how everyone - parents and players - approach the rounds.

The following table and statistics shared above are taken directly from *Every Shot Counts* (c) 2014 published by the Penguin Group and shared with expressed permission from the author, Mark Broadie. (I highly recommend this book - it is filled with powerful insights).

Distance (Feet)	One putt probability	Three putt probability	Average putts
2	99%	0.0%	1.01
3	96%	0.1%	1.04
4	88%	0.3%	1.13
5	77%	0.4%	1.23
6	66%	0.4%	1.34
7	58%	0.5%	1.42
8	50%	0.6%	1.50
9	45%	0.7%	1.56
10	40%	0.7%	1.61
15	23%	1.3%	1.78
20	15%	2.2%	1.87
30	7%	5.0%	1.98
40	4%	10.0%	2.06
50	3%	17.0%	2.14
60	2%	23.0%	2.21
90	1%	41.0%	2.40

And with that, I am hoping I made my first point with some degree of clarity - that in many cases we think we fail all because we are measuring ourselves against unrealistic expectations. Set reasonable goals and expectations, and your number of successes goes up.

Now, the second part of the story is how we all deal with the real failures - the days when the wheels fall off and the cart is in the ditch - whatever euphemism you choose. And just know it is going to happen and once you are on the train, you ride it for the 4.5 to 5 hour trip. And guess what? Although it sucks in that moment … and it feels like you want to just hit the eject button - something amazing is happening right before your eyes. As Maneet Chauhan shared, 'There are no failures in life: only learning opportunities'. The game of golf is hard and so dependent on so many different variables - a kid you saw shoot 68 yesterday may have slept in a weird position, may have woken up and gotten bad news about a

> "*There* **are** *no failures* **in life:** *only learning* **opportunities.**"
>
> –*Maneet Chauhan*

school project, or may have had a fight with a boyfriend or girlfriend before the round - all of which can serve to provide a Jekyll and Hyde scenario on the golf course and mean a 68 yesterday is an 82 today. Your kids will fail … they will hit it off the map, they will hit three in a row out of bounds, they will three putt from 10 feet (even though the table above says there is less than a 1% chance of doing so), and they will feel failure and disappointment. And in those moments, even though it hurts our hearts, we as the people who are 'this many years older than them' have to know and have to convey to them that this is a learning opportunity - this is a microcosm of life and it isn't about how many times we get knocked down, it is how many times we get back up. Just recently, we watched Ben as he was trying to chase down the leaders at a tournament (one of which is his best buddy) - he got into a 'spot of bother' (as you will often hear the announcers share at The Open Championship) and ended up making a double bogey. However, he bounced back and birdied the next two holes - He did not win the tournament but afterwards his mom got to him and said, 'that is what it is ALL about - bouncing back from adversity and not staying down'. Where did that bounce back come from? It came from countless rounds where we didn't bounce back … where we made a double, and then another - and then the parents (that being us) had the talk about how disappointments are learning opportunities as that they make us stronger for the next time, and the next time. See, kids think they are just playing golf ... but in reality, they are soaking up lessons that will serve them for the rest of their lives. Pretty cool, no matter what the statistics say.

Britt Said: Oh my goodness ... one of the hardest things to do is watch your child failing and you can't fix it. The quicker you learn it's just one day and one moment in time the better. We have often seen on the course one shot make a difference in Ben qualifying for a bigger event. It hurts like no hurt to see him hurt. I often want to fix it and make things right immediately, but it's out of my control. What I didn't see early on was the beauty of those missed shots. Those missed shots, missed cuts, and missed tournaments led to other good things. If I could give moms a piece of advice it would be to find something good in the days that are bad. I often say, 'today sucked', but you had fun with the guys you played with. Release the negative talk and celebrate the good and the bad. What matters is that your child feels loved on the good days and bad days. As parents we have to suck up our own emotions and pour love into our children to make them feel better about what has just happened. We are there to support them and not make them feel worse than they already do. As I've often heard from other parents, children don't mean to hit bad shots ... it just happens. Life is like that, too. We have good and bad days. We don't mean to make bad decisions, but we do. It's all in how we handle those decisions that build our character and lead us to making better decisions later. My goal is to teach Ben to look at the big picture and know that all things happen for a reason!

Mark wrote the poem below one day when he had some time to sit and reflect on a recent golf season, and we found that it did a pretty good job of capturing the journey through the eyes of the parents who watch and wait, who live and die with every swing. The fact that when some look at a score posted online, they will see just numbers - but the parents see, and know, and remember each part and piece that added up to that 4, or 5 or 7 - and how it was one more layer of experience for you, and for them.

Filling Boxes by Mark McKinney

An introspective look at the sport that is youth golf – and the emotional story that is painted from each tee box to each landing area where parents wait with bated breath to see their player's ball land safely – in bounds, on dry land, in a good lie. And as landing area shifts to green complex, the dance begins anew and life's lessons unfold – each of us and none of us having any power against what is to come – good or bad. And then there is the golfer – who – if he plays poorly is not sure who he has let down – himself, his parents, his coach, his teammates – or no one at all. He wonders if his score is his value, or his value his score. If he only knew, and if we only knew how best to tell him and more importantly, to show him.

Each box tells a story in and of its own
Only those who were present will know just what went on.

18 boxes once empty, now one by one are filled
some in angst, some in agony, and some are marked in thrill.

Yet, no one not present ever really knew
The anxiety that each box held for the athlete and their crew.

Was his heart so fast a beating that he could barely catch his breath?

Were his palms so sweaty, his hands so shaky that it must have felt like death?

Or, was his mind so clear, his focus so pure, that failure's not an option
Did he encounter a full onslaught of confidence adoption?

By shot and chip and putt and aim, you count them one by one

Until that ride is over, for a moment still, as that next box is done.

Then comes the next, a different test, another box to fill
Who's more nervous – him or you? Why can't our hearts be still?

We know the test is where they're forged, and from where they will emerge
If we will just let go and watch as preparation and life converge

It hurts to watch them when they fail, we wish that we could fix it
But knowing what we know we try to tell them 'just stick with it'.

A par, a par, and then a bogey, bogey run – you see it on his face and know the battle has begun. Has he failed himself or worse, does he think he just failed me? Oh how I wish that he could look inside and see how proud I be.

We're halfway through this roller coaster, fatigue is setting in - That's nine whole boxes, nine short stories and we walk our way towards Ten.

> The cycle keeps on going – a prayer before each swing – God help him to do HIS best and nothing in between – Don't protect him from adversity, cause that is where he grows – but when it comes, oh when it comes – please God make sure he knows. That he is stronger than he knows and one day he will see – the giant standing in his shoes – the man he wants to be.

It's lost so many times, I'm sure, as the boxes slowly fill – that the number in the boxes mean that each of them sure will – surely will miss the walk they share and the laughs and smiles and friendship – for we are so focused on those boxes that we even let out minds slip – 'you better make that next shot count' – this is life or death, or is it? As boxes fill and math takes over we let it pave the way – for how we feel about ourselves and how and what we say.

> The boxes just keep coming next, the hole count getting higher … the pencil marks are more and more, each tested by the fire. A tick mark here, a dot mark here to keep up with the day– but again for those that were not here, they'll never know the way – the way that 4 should have been a 6 if not for lucky bounces – or how that 6 could have been a 4, in other circumstances.

Each box holds a story, one eighteenth of a play – whose script is never written until the very day – until he steps upon that tee and grasps his trusty pen – and with heart a pounding, eyes 'a-glaze, sets it to paper once again. No script is ever quite the same – the twists and turns are special – some scripts are like a love story when everything goes right – and some are like a horror movie, where all there die that night.

But regardless of the story, once told it's told and sealed – for as the paper shows you, all the boxes are filled. And in each box, the lessons taught lie dormant there in wait – to see if he will take that box and use it to be great. Will he learn the lesson that God set upon his path – that He wove in from the very start and disguised as simple math.

We mustn't lose our sight along each 300-minute journey – we mustn't think that all our worth is tied up in a tourney. It's easy as a parent, a coach and as a player – to see success or failure as a life affirming layer – that if we win or play our best that somehow we are better – but tomorrow holds another script, whose boxes are unfettered. So careful must we be to never lose our focus – that this great game is just a game – and not let it define us.

Cause win or lose, succeed or fail in how he fills those boxes – it's our job as a parent to know, just what the true life crux is. That our job is to love him and to never let him doubt, that this does not define his worth – that's not what it's about. It's on us as his parents to help him clearly know, that the filling of the boxes – is how he learns to grow. That he is stronger than he knows and one day he will see – the giant standing in his shoes – the man he soon will be.

The Carrot and the Stick - What, When and How to Say It

'As parents, we wonder how to improve our relationship with our son or daughter daily. Sometimes things don't go easy, and we feel stuck. Nothing we do seems to work, and we search for different strategies. One of the secrets regarding youth sports parenting is about timing.

We want our kid to perform their sport and other activities according to our knowledge and set of skills. But, we have to realize they have their own pace and act accordingly. They need to experience failure to evolve and grow. Another thing regarding the topic is what to say and, more important when to say it. **Our words have a significant impact on them. They add or subtract, and they are never neutral.**

So, being wise to choose the right moment to speak is a must. But, unfortunately, we all feel tempted to deliver all the burden out of our minds and smash it to our kids. But we are far better than that. So, let's keep on improving our youth sports parenting skills.'

– HERNAN CHOUSA AUTHOR OF *PARENTSHIFT*

Mark Said: This section could require a psychology book all on its own because it is all about how we communicate with and motivate our kids when they do hit a funk and lose their focus. It still happens, even with all of the coaching, pep talks, etc - life is life and people are real ... and our emotions are powerful. Go to any junior golf tournament and you will see the continuum of parental psychology going on - depending upon how a player is playing at a particular moment. My biggest advice, the up don't stay up, and the down don't stay down. If a kid is playing 18 holes … the question of adversity is not IF but WHEN. And when the WHEN comes, you just hope and pray that the player is ready and equipped to deal with it … but sometimes, they just want to be in a funk and Eeyore around (if you don't know who Eeyore is, put this book down and go Google it).

When Eeyore does show up, there are several options we have as parents ... we can (1) ignore it and see if it works itself out, (2) we can be the carrot 'come on buddy, it is going to get better ... keep on plugging', or (3) we can be the stick ... and in our family, the stick takes the form of Britt with her teeth clenched mumbling something in hushed, yet audible tones, that only Ben can understand. It has become like something akin to sign language - and he knows that if he sees the teeth, he must really be acting 'some kind of way'.

We have learned the dance, as have so many parents, about when to be the carrot, when to be the stick - but what we have learned more than anything is that we don't have to try and fix every little situation. As I said before, these are kids, and they have to have an outlet when they are angry and frustrated - now ours knows that if that outlet were to include throwing anything, profanity of any kind, or disrespect to the course or fellow players we would all be in the vehicle heading home. But in all seriousness, it is important that they have a means of being angry because let's face it, this is the most frustrating game on the planet. I recall a tournament Ben played in at the beach and he hit a little rough patch, and we noticed that in between shots he was mumbling to himself and smacking his leg (a common outlet). Britt and I didn't think he was reacting like 'we' thought he 'should' so of course, we said something to him after the round, and he let us know that Tami (remember Tami) had let him know that it was OK to be upset between shots but never over a shot ... and by the way, that mumbling we had seen, it was him praying walking down the fairway for strength to reset. Open mouth, insert foot. All that to further remind us that relationships are complicated ... and we have to really know our kids and what makes them tick ... Sometimes they, like us, need the carrot and sometimes they need the stick - and sometimes, they need us to simply let them work it out on their own.

A word here, also, about the 'who' needs to be the carrot or the stick - sometimes it works for Britt to just show her teeth or clear her throat and more than anything now, it breaks the tension. But, more often and you will find this with tournament golf, the coach is the only one who can speak to the player and they, too, learn what works with each player. At a pretty big team event in the spring of 2021, Ben was rolling along through 3 holes and then the wheels came off ... and he found himself 6 over through 5 holes and went into a dark/disappointed/miserable place - it was on his face, in his body language everything - so we texted the coach and let him know that Ben needed a 'word'. His coach got to him and said, 'I don't care how you finish from this point out, but I want to see your head held high and your shoulders back and you walk with confidence on every step'. He played the next 13 holes in 4 under par just from that one exchange. It was the stick ... but it was the right stick, based on strategies that Tami shares about the importance of body language.

Britt said: I could use some therapy in this section myself. When Ben is struggling on the course and I see his head drop, I immediately tense up and want to shake him back into the real world. Sidenote: I've heard of shaken baby syndrome when parents become frustrated with babies, but if I could pick Ben up some days now ... he would have shaken teenager syndrome. If I've learned anything on the course it's that Mark and I both can't be mad at him at the same time. He has to have an out at some point. I know it seems we talk constantly to him, but we can't - we aren't allowed to. We can hand him drinks and food but coaching is not allowed. I wouldn't be much help in that area anyway. Knowing all this, sometimes Mark and I can see Ben begin to droop and be down (I can hear Tami right now saying 'focus on body language'). When I think he has had enough time to get himself together and he isn't ... I will tell Mark, 'You go on up ahead, I'm about to light him up!' As Mark goes ahead and after Ben hits his tee shot he will head over to walk to the next shot. With a big smile on my face and my teeth showing, I 'gently' remind him to get his act together.

> 'It can be hard not to show your emotions when you're watching your child play or to express your emotions after a competition. Children though are inherently sensitive to their parents' emotions. If you're showing disappointment or frustration at them, the officials, the coach, their teammates, etc. they will pick up on it and it can influence their feelings and behavior.
>
> Additionally, focusing on your negative emotions afterwards is detrimental. If they had a bad competition, had to deal with questionable calls, or their team made mistakes - you expressing yourself only intensifies their feelings. It could also make them feel powerless or even more frustrated.
>
> As Pete Carroll said, during and right after competition coaches and parents need to be the best cheerleaders or poker players'
>
> – Tami Matheny

My advice would be to talk about the round later, to laugh about the comments you made when you were gritting your teeth, and to make sure you don't embarrass your child in front of other children and parents. This will keep your emotions in check and not cause you to have a nervous breakdown right on the course. Another great tool I have come to use is the 'ignore it until they are coherent again' approach. Ben has, several times, told me after a bad round or in the heat of the moment to 'just pull me out of any other tournaments', or 'I just don't want to play anymore' … I don't take any of that 'in the moment' jibber jabber for real, and I wait until things have calmed down before we have that discussion. You will see in the **Pay Attention** section two instances where I did NOT do what he asked … and the plan unfolded just like it was supposed to. All my life I've heard the saying 'if you get knocked off the horse get right back up and ride again', I believe the same thing with the thoughts after a bad round of golf. Get back on the course and try to have a better round. Then decide after a good round if you still want to quit! I often remind Mark that neither of us gets over things quickly when we are mad, so how could we expect this child of ours to snap out of a funk immediately - when his parents struggle to do the same thing.

Mark said (a little more): Several parents I have come across have implemented the 24 hour rule - don't talk about anything about the round (or game) until 24 hours later, and I will admit that it provides a lot needed time and space to ensure that feedback is constructive, wanted, and delivered in a manner separated from the moment. I have been guilty of getting in the vehicle and wanting to throw everything at Ben I noticed right there in the moment, and it is unfair to him. Particularly on the bad days - I have to give him time to just 'be' and … I think that is the healthiest thing I can do as a dad. I have to remind myself of Hernan Chousa's words mentioned earlier about paying attention to your words, how you say it, when you say it, and why you say it. "...our words have a significant impact on them (kids). They add or subtract, and they are never neutral." Try the 24 hour rule ... it's tough ... but it's powerful.

> **'Be specific when you tell your child you are proud of them. Why are you proud of them goes a lot further than just saying you are proud'**
>
> – *Tami Matheny*

After that 24 hours - use your words in a conversation, not in a lecture. It has happened to me several times of late where I saw Ben hit a shot on the golf course over the green into trouble, and my 'in the moment' reaction wanted to be 'now why would you do that when you know there is trouble long?' I waited and in the right timing Ben said to me about one of those occasions 'Dad, did you see that shot I hit into 4 yesterday? It came out so low and I knew it had gone long as soon as I hit it - I was in a sand filled divot and side hill lie and just wanted to make sure I made good contact'. That is a microcosm of the dance between father and son, I think - we stand outside the ropes and don't have the benefit of Dave Feherty or Dottie Pepper telling us about the lie and conditions, and we make assumptions that this should be an 'easy shot'. Understand the golfer is doing their best in that moment - It is like a dad told me at a tournament as we walked down the fairways and talked about life in general - he said 'you know, we get upset when we see kids hitting shots off the map ... but, it is not like they MEANT to do it ... they didn't do it on purpose - so why should we get upset?'. Good old piece of humble pie, served piping hot right there by a stranger on a golf course.

We have a fellow golf mom who told me years ago 'He (Ben) is going to watch you and how you react', and I thought she was nuts. She was adamant, though, that she was correct, and I should pay attention to my body language, my facial expressions, and how I reacted to good and bad shots. 'Kids are watching the dads because they are looking to see if they have your approval or not - that is important to them'. It never hit more true than when I took a look at some of the comments in the survey in the **What the Kids Say** section a little later in this book.

It reminds me a lot of how we approach driving a car – I drive how I drive, and of course, I think I am the best at it frequently reminding my kids that 'I have been driving for 35 years ... so don't try to give me advice'. But, as soon as I ride somewhere with one of them, I start 'should-ing' them – you should drive slower, you should not tailgate, you should turn your blinker on sooner, you should have let that lady in, you should NOT have let that guy in, you should drive slower in the rain ... so on and so forth.

And the sobering fact of it all is, they drive like they see me drive. I get so caught up thinking I am the best at it and I have justification for every decision I make, and then I lambast them for doing the same when they are behind the wheel.

I think sports is a lot like that – it is so easy for us as parents to 'should' our kids as they play and practice – you should have taken the easy lay-up on that par 5 instead of going for it, you should not have let your frustrations show when you missed that putt, you should not have hit 7 iron when it was obviously an 8 iron shot, you should be practicing more wedge shots and you would not have missed that green ... so on and so forth.

And here comes the kicker ... we must look in the mirror and ask ourselves – how do we react and make decisions when put in similar situations? I never really paid attention to how much I 'should-ed' Ben until we went to play one day, and he was beating the brakes off of me ... and I was a bit frustrated because I was hitting it everywhere and was mumbling to myself, walking around in a funk. Ben said with all good intentions of helping his old man 'Your tempo is way too fast, and your ball position is so far back that you have no chance of hitting it where you are looking' – and my internal reaction was 'I've got this, just leave me alone and I will fix it'.

And then it hit me ... just like in the car ... when I was driving my actions and reactions were justified because, well, they were mine. But when one of the kids was driving, I got to 'should' them because I knew better than them. Just like that, I was doing the same thing on the golf course watching Ben – I constantly should-ed him.

The point is this – it is important to check ourselves at the door and look in the mirror to find out if the actions and reactions we see in our kids are a product of them watching us in similar situations. The strategy 'do as I say and not as I do' is weak, and I think, unfair to our kids in life and on the playing field.

Don't 'should' your kids.

Know the Why, and Stick to It

'Youth sports should be used as a platform to help kids build tons of skills and relationships that'll help them for life. Youth sports should NOT be used as a way for adults to feed their egos.'

– THE REFORMED SPORTS PROJECT

Mark said: As a dad, I can remember how excited I was when my daughter, Katie Britt, decided to play middle school basketball - I became an instant nut of a parent who wanted to pour all of the glory of my mediocrity into her through advice, drills and guidance during and after games. Katie Britt was quick to let us know she had no aspirations of ever pursuing athletics to any degree other than socially, and she was content being an awesome teammate and supporting from as far away from the floor as she could (just ask her, she will tell you).

I was just as excited when Ben first told me he wanted to play basketball, because I had another chance to tell someone all I knew about the sport - again, never a threat to play at the college level, but I understood the game and always felt like I had wisdom to share - if someone would just listen. Same with football - probably a lesser talent there for me in high school, but I had the standard things all dads have to teach their sons - run these routes, throw like this, catch like this, be tough, etc. Having played both sports, I fell into the old trap ... the V word ... the reliving of the glory days through the hands and feet of an 8-year-old. And if you are honest as a dad, you've probably been there before and are familiar with the V:

vi·car·i·ous·ly
/vəˈkerēəslē,vīˈkerēəslē/
adverb
1.   in a way that is experienced in the imagination through the
actions of another person.
"he/she was living vicariously through his/her children"

I think it may be hard wired into a dad from the word go - and if not controlled, it clouds any sort of vision and/or logical thoughts we may ever have when watching our kids play sports.

When Ben decided he wanted to start hitting golf balls, I was pumped. I had also played high school golf, not to any acclaim, and still play from time to time, although not able to capture the spark of my youth. I swore I would not fall into the same trap with golf as I had with football or basketball because this sport is super hard, super individual …super … yeah, it didn't work. As soon as I saw he had a natural knack for a golf swing, I made sure he had the right clubs, found someone to teach him the swing basics and found myself driving around the southeast to have him participate in Drive, Chip and Putt events when he was 9 years old. Looking back, I can see how much of a nut I really was - going to the facility of the DCP the evening before to make sure we could get a feel for the greens - wanting him to succeed so badly it hurt … entering him into tournaments and making sure we didn't miss an opportunity to play. Going over the round in the car on the way home to find out why we made a bogey on 12 or why we three putted on 17. And believe me, the better his golf swing got … the more 'Big V' I became - I could see he was going to easily surpass any level of talent I had on a golf course, and I embraced it.

I remember vividly when we signed him up in a junior golf series run by Mr. Mike Carlisle, long time golf coach at USC Aiken – we had no clue how it all worked. We had pushcart, clubs, snacks, etc … and

I had always been with Ben when we played, and we would choose clubs together … me guiding him. I remember asking Coach Carlisle on the first tee 'so what interaction can we have with the kids?' and he said 'none – they do everything on their own … let them learn, have fun, and enjoy playing - follow along, but meet them when they come off the last green.'

And in that moment, I said to myself *'this isn't fair … he doesn't know how to … what if he … I have to be there to tell him … '.* But it didn't matter, those were the rules. And we watched as Ben hit shots, made decisions … failed, succeeded, and Britt and I lived and died with every shot. We got into scoring disputes with other parents over whether a kid had an 8 or a 7 … and we did everything we could to ensure Ben had what he needed to play his best. I still have a piece of paper I stuck to his pull cart when he was 9 … 9 years old … and this thing had more instructions than an airplane emergency landing procedure – but I thought I was helping him. I thought that it mattered if he shot 44 on nine holes versus 47. That the 5-footer he missed for par on hole 7 really was going to make a difference.

I also remember when he was just starting out – and we were shooting 47 on nine holes, I saw other kids shooting 38, 37 … 36 – and I said – why can't 'WE' be doing that. And I did it … the thing you should never do as a parent – I began to compare my kid to another and derive my happiness out of how well Ben did relative to another kid. And I said to myself, 'hey, if we can get to where we can break 40 consistently … I will be happy'. We did, and I wasn't. I moved on … 'If we can shoot in the 30s consistently … I will be happy'. We did, and I wasn't. Then we moved to 18-hole tournaments as he got older … and the process started all over again. Golf parents know once you move up to the 18-hole tournaments you find yourself as the youngster playing with the older kids, and courses are longer, tougher, etc until you begin to get stronger. So here we were … 85, 86, 87 … and I said 'hey, if we can start shooting 80 consistently – I will be happy'. We did, and I wasn't. The story continues …. If we can shoot in the 70's, mid 70's, low 70's … at or near even … under par.

> 'My kids are 23 and 21. As Father's Day approaches I'm reflecting on my journey as a Dad. One mistake I made as a parent was I put too much pressure on them. At times they felt my expectation but not enough connection. I got better as they got older but wish I did things different when I was younger. I can't change my past but hope this helps you or someone you know. It's why I'm passionate about positive leadership and why I've become a good teacher. I've made mistakes and learned what doesn't work and what does. I recently was asked what I wished I would have done different. Here are a few:
>
> - Focusing on the moment instead of what's next.
> - Supporting them instead of giving advice.
> - More trust and less fear.
> - Asking what they want to do instead of telling them what they should do.
> - Focus more on happiness than success.
> - Let them figure it out instead of figuring it out for them.
> - Just bringing calm energy instead of tense anxious energy.'
>
> *–Jon Gordon*

The story was always the same – no matter what milestone we were chasing – and we found, as a family, that our moods ... our collective moods were all driven by how Ben played on a particular day. And often it was how well he played relative to other kids .... If we had a bad day, but we also knew several others did as well ... then our moods lightened. If we had a bad day and everyone else played well ... then the silence, awkward drives home, meals eaten where we didn't want to talk about anything relative to golf ensued.

Looking back now so many years and thousands of golf shots later ... I realize Coach Carlisle was absolutely right, and I was absolutely wrong. I got so tied up in the dad part of it – the 'I am going to equip and prepare my son to be the best' that I missed so much and in doing so, took so much away from Ben's experience. It's a lot like those people, and I have been guilty of it, who cannot enjoy the experience for wanting to take out a phone and video it or take a picture to capture the experience. Forest and the trees ... whatever you want to use to describe it - it's all the same.

In hindsight, as I look back now at our Junior in high school - it is hard sometimes to remember who wanted it more - him or me. I can remember conversations as a family early in high school golf whereby I would ask Ben if he wanted to play competitive golf still, or not - usually after a bad round where I felt he could have done better - and sitting here as I write this, I know now I didn't want to hear his answer - I simply wanted to hear him say 'yes, I want to play competitive golf and continue to work hard to get better.'

What I also know now, is that I am darn lucky he didn't just say 'to heck with it' and decide to play something else or nothing at all. I can honestly say he has a genuine passion for the game, playing with his buddies and teammates and has a drive and a vision to play collegiate golf someday, and that is what drove him to stick with it. Not that I think he ever resented me for pushing him, but I do know it took me realizing it myself - that I was in fact living vicariously through him - in order for me to let go and let him turn into the player he is becoming.

'For some reason, adults - some who can't even kick a ball - think it's perfectly ok to scream at children while they're playing soccer. How normal would it seem if a mother gave a six-year-old some crayons and a coloring book and started screaming, 'Use the red crayon! Stay in the Lines! Don't use yellow!? Do you think that child would develop a passion for drawing?'

– CLAUDIO REYNA, US SOCCER HALL OF FAME

Perhaps the most tangible transformation that took place across my realization of how much I was trying to control the situations was the range time before events. In the beginning, I was there for his warm-ups 95/5 - I talked to him about the course, about his swing, watched each practice swing and offered guidance for poorly struck ones (little did I know, I was ratcheting up the stress for both of us) ... as I transitioned through this learning process of being the best and most supportive dad I could be, I watched that mix go from 95/5 to 80/20 to 40/60 ... and ultimately where it sits today - probably 5/95 (and I will only go to the range now if he texts me to say he needs something or has a question. Now, he drives himself to tournaments when he can, and we show up a little before tee time). In doing so, the stress is so much less because I now know his 'Why' is for the love of the game, and not playing to please me. As simple as that sounds - it is a freeing feeling for both of us - for our entire family (early on, in the 95/5, I would report to Britt after each range session and say things like 'it's gonna be a long day, he's not hitting it solidly' which then freaked her out … and it set a completely stressful tone for the day). Embrace their Why and let it remain their Why. Make sure your Why is for their love of the game or something similar.

Britt said: We've always told Ben if he wanted to play, we would do all we could to support him - financially and emotionally - and that if he ever wanted to stop, all he had to do was tell us - it is not our rodeo. However, on one particular tournament day in recent years, Ben had a bad stretch of holes and got into an absolute funk -

'Parents, your children can't give you life. They can't give you sturdy hope. They can't give you worth. They can't give you peace of heart. They can't give you right desires and motivation. They can't give you strength to go on. They can't give you confidence and courage in the middle of a trial. And they can't give you that ultimate, heart-satisfying love that you long for. I'm going to say it in a way that I hope will get your attention. It just never works to ask your children to be your own personal saviors. This is a burden they will never bear well, and it will introduce trouble and struggle into your relationship with them. Jesus is your life, and this frees you and your children from the burden of asking them to give you what your Savior has already given you.'

–Pastor Paul David Tripp

which he knows crawls all over us as parents (the funk part, not the bad stretch). When I was able to talk to Ben after the round, he said 'I feel like if I play bad, y'all don't love me', and we realized as a team, his team of parents, that if he truly felt that way, we had let him down. It created an opportunity for a very honest and open dialogue that was much needed in our family, and it changed the way we talk about, plan for, and support each other at a golf tournament. Ben felt when he saw us upset it was because his score was not as good as it should be - when in reality, we were upset that his attitude had tanked, and he was letting one bad break or shot lead to another because his mind was cluttered with being ticked off. The difference can be very subtle, and in an environment where you can't readily chat-it-up to explain in the moment - it all comes down to reading body language - and therein lies room for confusion. My point is this - as parents, we make our kids feel some kind of way and it is typically driven when our whys are not aligned - at that point, in that tournament if only for a brief moment, Ben's Why shifted to 'because mama and daddy are upset if I don't do well'. If the Why is not because 'they want to play', then we are certainly headed for rough waters. If the Why has anything to do with 'because I know that is what you all want me to do' - it is time for an open discussion and reevaluation of priorities. Truth be told, I think there were times when Ben did play for us versus playing for himself and the love of the game, and shame on us for not recognizing it sooner.

A very dear friend of mine shared the following story with me recently, and I was struck at how well it speaks to the importance of the Why and even more importantly, to the importance of having real conversations with our children - no matter what age.

'My wife and I were sitting with our kids during early spring discussing the activities coming up for this sports season. My daughter (7) had played two years of softball and my son (9) had been playing baseball for five years. While my daughter seemed to be really enjoying it, my son had struggled keeping up with the talent growth of his friends the last couple of years and seemed to have lost the excitement he had a few years back. We asked our daughter if she would like to play softball and she said "Yes!" right away. She wanted to go out that night and throw the softball in the yard to get ready. We asked our son if he wanted to play baseball and he said, "Sure." with very little enthusiasm.

Knowing how the last couple of years had been for him, I asked him if he really wanted to play. I told him there were other things in the spring he could do like soccer or track, he didn't have to play baseball. He looked up at me with a confused look on his face and said "Wait, I don't have to play baseball?" I said "Of course not. You can do whatever sport you want." Then he said something that I will never forget. He said "You always talk about baseball, and I've always played it, so I thought I had to. I didn't know I had an option."

My heart sank. I never wanted to be one of those dads who force their kids to do something but here I was. I didn't do it from a "you are going to be a superstar" or "you have to be better than so and so", I did it subconsciously out of fear of getting out of MY comfort zone. I told him "Son, if you never pick up a bat the rest of your life, I'm okay with that. You do what you want to do. Not what you think will make Mom and I happy." Then with a look of relief, he said "I don't want to play baseball. My friends and I play soccer during recess, and I want to try doing that." So that year, he played soccer. We had no idea what any of the rules were or how to set up the positions. All I know is he wanted to play. He was not the best or most talented, but he loved every second of it. And for the first time in a long time, I saw my son playing a sport and smiling.'

Let the player lead you where they want to go – some want to compete, some want to play (and some would rather fish - true story, a young man told Ben in the second fairway of a pretty big tournament 'man, I'd rather be on the lake fishing right now.'). The Why can't be ours - it can't be for scholarships or bragging rights …or so that our ego gets to be boosted for the day … it cannot be anything to do with us … It has to be about the child. My challenge to you as a parent reading this book - *ask your player why they play the game and be prepared to talk honestly about it* - the sooner you all know the why, the easier the road ahead will be.

A really powerful resource we came across in our research of this book and subsequent introduction to Ryan Dailey and Matt Reagan, co-Founders of Operation 36 Golf, is their Junior Development Model. Operation 36 leverages data and analytics, but also the ever-critical inputs from the junior golfer as to what their goals are (i.e., their Why) to help everyone get and stay on the same page relative to 'where is this journey going?'.

Here is a brief description of the tracks Operation 36 identifies (taken directly from their website at https://operation36.golf/junior-golf-development-model/.)

- Exploratory Track - I want to try out the sport and see if it is for me (preferably with friends).

- Social Track - I like being at the course with my friends and want to get comfortable playing.
- Recreational Track - I like playing golf and find enjoyment in trying to improve my skills.
- Competitive Track - I want to take my skills and start competing against others in tournaments.

I know our family would have been well served to have come across these resources 10 years ago and likely saved ourselves a lot of heartache, headache, and stress. This is an amazing team doing powerful work, and we are blessed to have met them. *(Spoiler Alert: Check out Ryan's guidance to parents and juniors in Advice from People Who Know)*

'Just because a kid doesn't want to or isn't good enough to play sports in college doesn't mean their athletic experience isn't as important to them as a kid who's destined for an athletic scholarship. Playing sports can save a kid's life. We can't forget that.'

–The Reformed Sports Project founder Nick Buonocore

It's All Fun and Games Until Someone Gets Hurt

'...parents, though, play the biggest supporting role. No relationship shapes our entire lives more than our relationships with our parents. Parents set the tone in whether their children become excuse makers or problem solvers. Whether they rise above adversity or fall to it.'

– ANONYMOUS

Mark said: This is perhaps the toughest chapter for me to write because it shines a light and points a finger at the mistakes I made as a dad on this journey. My dad always said, *'you don't know how you look til you get your picture took,'* and that remains true in this case. I always convinced myself at tournaments I was the sane dad - the one who got a little stressed, true, but at least I didn't act like 'that guy' or throw a fit like 'that lady'. I could justify my mood changes when Ben would start playing poorly … similar to an addict, I suppose - I thought no one could read me and tell my demeanor changed in direct proportion to how things were going on the course. Enter Britt who was dead straight honest with me and told me I was a little 'much' and I really needed to control my emotions and be aware of how closely my attitude, my mood, was related to Ben's golf score. I had told myself it did not - I had even self-talked myself into believing I only cared about his happiness and that he was enjoying himself. I was lying to myself and to my family, and thought I was getting away with it.

Then it hit me one day, somewhere in the middle of Ben's sophomore year in high school how insane this cycle was. How many hours I had wasted being mad about something I could not control – how I was getting my joy based on how well he played. It hit me because in 2020, Britt and I lost our 24-year-old nephew, Cole (her brother's son), in a tragic plane crash, and I found myself thinking if his parents could snap their fingers and have him back – they wouldn't care WHAT his golf score was on a given day – they would just want more time. And like a light switch being flipped, I changed my perspective which has been a much healthier approach. Oh, I still get nervous and found myself unable to even speak to Ben before he teed off in the state championship this year (2021), but I now watch with the understanding this is a blessing I get to enjoy, and I would be well served to soak it all up.

The scariest part of all of this – as nuts as it sounds – is I run into 'me' on the golf course every week we play, and I have found that we, the golf dads, are like some dysfunctional group of misfits who are truly in need of a support group before and after every round. And the more I noticed the 'mes' on the course and witnessed the in-round, post-round discussions between fathers and sons ... the gritted teeth, the arguments back and forth, the dad storming off after a missed putt or bad decision – the more I realized 'hey, a large percentage of us are not equipped to deal with this in a healthy way' – and I have no doubt about that statement.

In other words, I am not the lone ranger – there are a lot of dads out there who get just as keyed up as I do ... we all just ride different horses. As well, we like to compare ourselves to each other – 'well, I may have been ticked off ... but at least I didn't tell my son to sell his clubs' or 'at least my son didn't cuss me when he walked off the course' or 'if my son ever said that to me ... boy, he'd be walking home'. I've heard them all ... and if you hang around junior golf enough, you will as well. In the upcoming chapter **The Dads You'll Meet** (hint: you may be one (*or more*) of them. It's like one of those Cosmopolitan Magazine quizzes come to life) - we are hoping you get a laugh and perhaps have the chance to self-identify to see which one (or maybe more) apply to you.

I would be remiss if I didn't speak to the times a parent will have to caddie for their player, which, on the surface seems like a match made in heaven. Be careful here as I (big surprise) botched this one more than a time or two. Our player/caddie relationship was awesome in that we got to both be 'inside the ropes' together and spend the 5 hours walking, talking, laughing and being father-son. The issue came in, at least for us, when I 'shoulded' Ben over and over - I made the mistake of not realizing this young man's talents vastly exceeded mine - so when he would say 'I am going to hit this shot' I would often, knowing in my mind there was no way I could pull that off, try to steer him away from it. I recall, and Ben will as well, a specific incident with a greenside shot he wanted to chip, and I felt (knowing there was no way I could get the chip shot that needed to be played close) that he should putt it - being a teenager and knowing his dad was telling him to do something, he chose my route - it did not work.

Later when we talked about it, it was very clear why. In golf, we have to be fully committed on each shot - in that moment, Ben saw the shot he wanted to play and believed it was correct. When I told him my opinion, even though he disagreed with it he went along with it but was not committed, because he was only doing it to please me. Long story short, if I could go back in my time machine THIS is one the things I would want a do-over on so I could keep my mouth shut, tell him his yardage, and hand him the club HE asked for. Don't miss the point(s) here because as a parent, both mom and dad, you will have the opportunity to caddie. My best advice if you choose to do it, recognize that this is for THEM and not for YOU. Don't 'should' your player and the walk will be a lot more enjoyable.

I recently re-read the *Golf Digest* article, *Golfer Learns That Father Doesn't Always Know Best* by Steve Elling from December 2004 documenting the strained relationship that Sean O'Hair, former youth golf sensation and PGA Tour Professional, had with his father. Pause here a moment and go give that a Google and a read … and let that perspective wash over you if you think the parent/athlete relationships don't matter.

Britt said: Every child is different and as parents we sometimes don't realize the impact our words and actions have on children. In my opinion, Ben was hardheaded, stubborn, and unruly as a little boy. I threatened him with his life and realized the only thing that truly mattered to him was a wooden spoon. He could proudly wear the 'I survived the wooden spoon' shirt that is seen all over the internet today. It was hard at first because we had one child who I could look at and make cry, and then, we had Ben. I learned to buy a purse big enough to carry a spoon with me. I can still open a kitchen drawer to this day when he is being sassy, and he will immediately stop and give me a wry smile. He finally believed me when I had to spank him with the spoon. It got his attention. It made memories, and Butch, my daddy, never spoke a truer statement as he used to say tongue in cheek of course, 'He needs his a$$ whipped every day when he wakes up'.

What I didn't realize during all this was he also has one of the most tender hearts I have ever seen. He is like me in that we get our feelings hurt a lot. Statements are made or actions are seen, and we don't forget them. We often carry things from one day to the next with people and they don't even realize they have hurt us. As parents we have to be careful with what we say and do with our children. Yes, they need correcting and shouldn't be allowed to throw clubs, curse, or act foolish on the golf course, but the children also need the opportunity to let us know when they are hurting. We have to realize our feelings may be hurt, but we can't impose more pain on the child by our comments or actions. The old saying 'if you can't say something nice, don't say anything at all' applies here.

Coming to the realization that what we do and what we say matters is crucial as parents. Whether you are threatening the child with a wooden spoon or allowing the child to express in words the feelings and emotions being experienced, we have to remember that everything matters. Children don't forget and they remember the things that impact them - both good and bad.

When I think about the times that Mark and Ben have been in the silent treatment zone, it makes me think about the story below - *Holes in the Fence.*

HOLES IN THE FENCE (UNKNOWN)

There is a story about a young boy who had difficulty managing his temper. One day his father had an idea. He gave the boy a bag of nails and a hammer and said, "Every time you feel like lashing out at someone or having a tantrum, I give you permission to pound a nail into the backyard fence." Over the next several weeks, the boy did just that. The first few days he hammered a constellation of nails into the first panel. Then, gradually, panel-by-panel, nail-by-nail, he slowed down until he found that he didn't need to do it anymore.

That was when his father gave him a new challenge: to remove a nail from the fence for every day he could continue to control his temper. Eventually, all the nails were removed, and the son stood proudly before his father.

"That's great," the father said, "But I want you to notice something. Look at those holes in the fence. Those holes don't go away when you take the nails out. It's the same thing when you say or do something hurtful to someone else; you can try to take it back later, but the damage remains."

"When this happens it's easy to say, "I'm just a passionate person – it's just the way I am," and hope that people will forgive you for your emotional outbursts. In many cases people will forgive you, especially if they have some history with you and trust you. But always remember that each time you do that, you are leaving another hole in the fence."- Imtiaz Manj

Perhaps the single most important thing you will take away from this experience is contained in the powerful words that will be shared in the following sentences. While reading, we challenge you to take a hard look at yourself and be honest with the same - I know we have been 'those people' and this article could have been taken from an interview with our family on a quiet ride home from a tournament. It's another one of those sobering moments - but at the same time, most powerful with the ability to transform relationships. Curious? Read on and see what Bruce E. Brown and Rob Miller of Proactive Coaching LLC had to say on the subject all the way back in 2012. We have included only a portion of the article below but encourage you to read it in its entirety. In addition, you can learn more about the work of Bruce and Rob at https://proactivecoaching.info/shoppac/.

Content below is shared with permission from ThePostGame.com and the article can be read in its entirety at the link provided below:

http://www.thepostgame.com/blog/more-family-fun/201202/
what-makes-nightmare-sports-parent

WHAT MAKES A NIGHTMARE SPORTS PARENT AND WHAT MAKES A GREAT ONE

BY: STEVE HENSON - 2/15/2012

Hundreds of college athletes were asked to think back: "What is your worst memory from playing youth and high school sports?"

Their overwhelming response: "The ride home from games with my parents."

The informal survey lasted three decades, initiated by two former longtime coaches who over time became staunch advocates for the player, for the adolescent, for the child. Bruce E. Brown and Rob Miller of Proactive Coaching LLC are devoted to helping adults avoid becoming a nightmare sports parent, speaking at colleges, high schools and youth leagues to more than a million athletes, coaches and parents in the last 12 years.

Those same college athletes were asked what their parents said that made them feel great, that amplified their joy during and after a ballgame. Their overwhelming response: "I love to watch you play."

There it is, from the mouths of babes who grew up to become college and professional athletes. Whether your child is just beginning T-ball or is a travel-team soccer all-star or survived the cuts for the high school varsity, parents take heed.

> **What if your child came to your place of business and watched you work all day and said 'Dad, why didn't you call that person back yet?' - 'Mom, should you have printed that presentation in color' - 'Mom, why didn't you say 'this' in the meeting?' - 'Dad, you made dumb decisions all day not sure why you still have a job.'**

The vast majority of dads and moms that make rides home from games miserable for their children do so inadvertently. They aren't stereotypical horrendous sports parents, the ones who scream at referees, loudly second-guess coaches or berate their children. They are well-intentioned folks who can't help but initiate conversation about the contest before the sweat has dried on their child's uniform.

In the moments after a game, win or lose, kids desire distance. They make a rapid transition from athlete back to child. And they'd prefer if parents transitioned from spectator – or in many instances from coach – back to mom and dad. ASAP. Brown, a high school and youth coach near Seattle for more than 30 years, says his research shows young athletes especially enjoy having their grandparents watch them perform.

"Overall, grandparents are more content than parents to simply enjoy watching the child participate," he says. "Kids recognize that."

A grandparent is more likely to offer a smile and a hug, say "I love watching you play," and leave it at that.

We couldn't have said it better ourselves and are thankful for this resource that puts into words what is sometimes so difficult to find the words to explain (we encourage you to read the article in its entirety - it's powerful). Get in the habit of using those magic words … I love to watch you play; I know we have.

The Dads You'll Meet

'10% of conflicts are due to differences of opinion. 90% are due to the wrong tone of voice.

— UNKNOWN

Britt said: Time for a little breather and what we hope is comic relief - although they say there is truth in humor. I am taking the lead on this because sometimes it is hard for men to see themselves ... well, as they are (just kidding, we love you guys). This list was compiled and written by a fellow golf parent, Eric Smith, whose son has played with Ben and crew for many years now. We get to see them several times a year at tournaments, and we look forward to the laughs and the stories almost as much as the golf.

We came across this list during a round in which our two boys got paired together, and we found ourselves huddled around Eric's phone late in the round as he read them aloud to us - and we laughed - but secretly, I was looking at Mark saying 'hmm, hmm ... I have seen you be all or most of these at some point'. We find ourselves now 'diagnosing' the dads we play with, and oh yes, I diagnose Mark in-round as well, to see which one of these folks we are with on a given day.

Golf Fathers (not to be confused with Godfathers) contributed by Eric Smith

The Best Friend Dad – The best friend dad or BFD is a right cheerful chap that is all up in your business asking questions about you, your son/daughter, and every aspect of your life so happy and exuberant ... that is until his son/daughter makes a double or triple bogey, he then becomes Loner Dad ... The poor child of a BFD often faces the dad's wrath on the ride home (sometimes while still on the course) of everything that went wrong during the round.

The Past Tour Pro Dad – The past tour pro dad or PTPD (not to be confused with PTSD although most golf dads have some form of PTSD). This is a very interesting dad for sure, he's the guy that lets you know right up front that he's a very accomplished golfer in his own right, he touts how he's played mini tour events and even tried the coveted Monday qualifying for the NIKE/WEB.COM/Korn Ferry/ whatever tour ... he touts his very impressive club championship career and how his son/daughter is a chip off the old block ... that is right up to the point their child makes 5 bogeys in a row followed by the dreaded quadruple bogey ... at this point you usually see him headed for the clubhouse for an adult beverage to calm his nerves.

The Over Expressive Dad – The OED is also known as the edge of the seat dad ... He is the dad that lives and dies by every swing of the club. He is generally easy to spot since he is the one with his hands in the air when his child misses a 5-footer for par that had a foot of break or the one doing fist pumps when their child makes that tough 2-footer for birdie ... He is overly happy when his child hits one in close and ready to bite someone's head off when they miss that 2-footer for par ... This dad is not to be confused with the BFD since this dad's 100% focus is on his child and there is little to no interaction with anyone else on the planet, they have no time for small talk, they are way too busy channeling positive thoughts and powers into their child, you know the hands in the air when they miss that 4-foot birdie putt or 3 putts from 8 feet … I know we have all seen him … especially when we look in the mirror, because we have all been this dad at some point.

The Too Cool Dad – The TCD dad is the dad that you see hanging out in the lobby or the hotel bar having a few (or way) too many "adult beverages". This dad typically shows up at the course the next morning in flip flops (the shoe of choice for walking 18 holes of golf) because tying shoes is tough to do when the world is spinning around so fast … When he arrives at the course, he makes a beeline for the coffee and the bathroom, all at the same time … He typically shows up after the first few holes since the bathroom break took way longer than expected … At this point he's impervious to what's happening on the course but you can bet the child will find out what went wrong with their round when they get in the car … some of the stories that seem to leak out about this dad and his antics, whew… and sometimes it leaks out on the course, and when it does… ouch!

The Loner Dad – The LD is the guy that shows up on the first tee with their child then slips along by themselves the entire round, sometimes you can even spot them slipping through the woods watching their child from afar. When you see this dad head for one of the bathrooms or the clubhouse it can be interesting listening to some of the conversations they have with themselves when they think no one is close by … Yep, ole LD will be busy as a bee talking to himself about how dumb of a decision it was for their child to not layup on that par 5, or how inept they are for missing that 3 foot put for bogey … Heck one time I witnessed an LD walk up to his son after he finished the first hole of a tournament to tell him "Boy you are too dumb to play golf"… The LD slowly walked back to his golf cart, got in, turned around and drove off not to be seen the rest of the day … My guess is he caught up with Too Cool Dad for a few cold ones, but that's just speculation.

The fact of the matter is, at some point we have all been probably 3 or 4 of these dads and in some cases all during the same round of golf or at least the same tournament. I once read a book about how to be a supportive dad for kids playing sports … a few months later in a tournament, my son and I had the pleasure to play a competitive round of golf with the author of the book and his son. He was caddying for his son, and I was caddying for my son. I thought, 'oh man I am going to get to see how it is done here, maybe I can learn something today.' The trouble started on about the 7th hole when the kid (a very good golfer) made a bogey, then another, then another, until finally a double bogey on the 12th hole upset the entire apple cart and ended with the dad yelling at his son and his son throwing up beside the green. I thought 'hmm … I think page 36 paragraph 3 deals with this issue, why did he not apply it to this situation' then I said to myself, looks like most other dads I have seen … It is tough for any parent that has kids playing sports, especially one who plays an individual sport.

The fact is golf is an extremely hard sport and an individual sport at that. The mental aspect of golf takes its toll on the kids and the parents. It is a high stress atmosphere where the kids typically put more stress on themselves than we realize. This brings me to the rarest of all golf dads … he is a unicorn in his own right and out of my nearly 10 years of being on the Junior Golf Circuit as the dad and Sponsor's Exemption, I have only seen one or two of these dads. He is the Supportive Dad (could also stand for Sasquatch Dad since they are both that rare) or SD for short. Now most of us have been this dad at one point in time and maybe I mistook the one or two that I have seen by only seeing a snapshot of someone, but I do not think this is the case. The SD is the dad that keeps the same demeanor all the time, through the good and the bad, telling the child it is ok, it is only golf (which sometimes makes the child mad) but the dad just keeps his same demeanor. This is the dad we all should strive to be, but we get so wrapped up in our own world that we get in our own way, and WE pile on even more stress on a child that is trying their level best to impress their dad … and somehow the kids still love us afterwards … I have witnessed kids, even kids that seemed distant from their parents, always look at their dad when they make a good shot or miss a putt. They look at them for support, encouragement and hopefully seeing their dad be proud of them. Oh, how many times I have screwed this up while watching my son.

I know for a fact I have fallen short way too many times of being the kind of dad that I should have been and should be. I want my son to look back on this time years from now and think of it as 'wow, that was a lot of fun, I would do all of it over again.' At the end of the day, it is not about the score, it is not about impressing other parents or players or friends, it is about strengthening our kids as being upstanding young men and women that has a higher ethical code than others since they are held to such high standards of ethics by the rules of golf. I know, I know, I have seen kids (a few, not a lot) cheating countless times in tournaments but you look at the pressure that is being put on them by their parents in some cases, it is easy to see why they would cheat.

Britt said: In addition to the dads Eric highlighted above, I have kept my own notes that I secretly use to diagnose Mark during a round and then later rib him on the way home. Some of mine will be a play off of Eric's above, but I like to put my own spin on things.

Disappearing Dad - We saw this dad just a couple of tournaments ago - he met us on the first fairway, and we did the normal introductions, where are you from, which one is your child - type of things. He was as polite as he could be, and we enjoyed the discussion ... and then, it all changed when his son who had parred the first 5 holes had a bogey, then another bogey, then a double ... and he became more and more agitated to the point that after the boys teed off on hole 9, he never slowed down when he hit the green, and we didn't see him again until the 18th green when he popped out to ask 'What is my son putting for now?' and when we told him he had been putting for par but missed it to bogey the final hole ... he pulled the disappearing act again.

This Game Shouldn't be Hard Dad - When Mark and I started dating, he spent more time with my daddy (remember Butch from earlier) than he did with me because they played golf all the time. So, I decided to take up the game so that I didn't get left out. I share that to say this - this is a hard game, and I know that just from the little that I played over the years. Which brings me to the This Game Shouldn't be Hard Dad - the man has never been a player himself but is involved because his son or daughter has a talent for the game and yammers on about how dumb it was for their child to miss a green from an obviously easy position. They have no clue - no idea, and I have decided that in most cases, it's just not worth the conversation to try and explain it.

Energizer Bunny Dad - Similar to Erics' OED above, I describe the Energizer Bunny Dad as the one that just cannot stop moving given all of their nervous energy. Mark is super guilty here ... knuckle popping, adjusting clothes, pacing - anything to stay in motion. There is another dad that we play with who matches and most often exceeds

Mark's energy level and we joke that if we could get a wire hooked to both of them, they could power a small city.

Touchdown Jesus Dad - We have only seen this one once, but he made such an impact on us that we just had to include him. This man's son had struggled off the tee for the better part of 13 holes - could not buy a fairway - so when he finally hit one down the middle on 14, the dad popped out of his cart and into the fairway with both hands raised above his head and shouted, "TOUCHDOWN JESUS!!"

We are Selling the Clubs Dad - My heart always hurts when I see a dad berating a child right there for everyone to see over something that happens on the golf course. We have witnessed and heard about dads shouting things like 'we are selling your clubs when we get done', 'you don't deserve to be out here' to the ultimate of just outright shouting matches across fairways. Talk about a car ride home, huh?

I Don't Have a Clue Dad - Sometimes I find myself jealous of this dad because in all honesty, they don't have a clue - and don't want to have a clue. They know that their child loves the game and wants to play it, but they have no desire to figure out the rules or try to grasp the complexities. They serve their child by being there to support them ... but have markedly less stress than anyone else because they don't really get the fact that penalty strokes, out of bounds markers and such are things to be feared. They are oblivious and yet, content.

On Restriction Dad - You will see several dads at tournaments who will fist bump their son or daughter pre-round and then turn to leave the course or go hang out somewhere on site until the round is over. We have come to learn that some of these dads have actually been put on restriction by either the child or the mom (or both). Players have said 'I can't take having you watch me play because you get so keyed up,' so dad serves out his restriction the best way he knows how. I will admit that Mark was on restriction sometimes early on - he would work himself into a frenzy, and it drove us all crazy. Ben spoke up for him, though, and said that he wanted him back - and they both joke with me now about knowing they need to behave so that they don't get put on punishment again.

How To Navigate It All
(The Kitchen Drawer)

'Circumstances have no power over you. One day traffic bothers you. One day you are in a great mood and it doesn't. It's not the traffic. It's not the event. It's always your state of mind.

−JON GORDON

Mark said: This is perhaps the most fun chapter to write because it is almost a stream of consciousness of all of those things we'd try to tell you if we have dinner together and you asked about those little things, the things you may have never thought to ask - this is the advice equivalent of that drawer ... 'that' drawer in your kitchen that has extra keys, matches, sticky notes, your son's 3rd grade report card, the business card from the plumber you used 7 years ago, the menu for the restaurant that went out of business ... toothpicks, Lord knows 1,000,000 toothpicks, sudoku puzzles, black tape, scotch tape, duct tape, glue, battery charger ... and that's just the front half. We all have that drawer, so ain't no shame in our game, and below is our version of that drawer in terms of parental advice. Some we may have mentioned before, but that's ok because we know we are getting older.

Britt said: Realize you will likely make dinner plans around who plays well, who plays poorly ... so the table for 12 may become a table for 4 ... and that's OK. Be prepared to adjust on the fly.

Britt said: Choose kindness, always. To the parents who aren't like you, to the players who irritate you - be nice.

Mark said: You <u>WILL</u> play in 35 degree weather, in 100 degree weather, in 30 mph winds, in pea soup fog, and the bugs will bite. Bundle up, strip down, hang on, do your best to see, cover up with bug spray - and enjoy every minute of it.

Britt said: As with all travel sports you will find as parents, we sacrifice a lot - none of these pursuits is inexpensive, so we find ourselves foregoing a true vacation so that we can go to a tournament somewhere. Oftentimes, we get lucky and find ourselves at the coast and sneak in some beach time ... but just know it is indeed a sacrifice but one I know we would not change for a minute.

Britt said: Be aware of the impact your focus on your junior athlete can have on other children in the family. As Hernan Chousa points out in Parentshift - it is important to pour into all of your children and ensure that they feel the same amount of love and support and that you have proper family balance. For our daughter, Katie Britt, this project helped us realize how much of a trooper she has been. Luckily for us, she loves being right there on the fairway with the family watching Ben and being part of the overall village.

Mark said: Further to the relationship Katie Britt, our daughter, has with Ben - she provides an important outlet for him when he may not want to talk to Britt and myself. He can tell her things about how he feels and what he needs on a different level - and for any Seinfeld fans out there, you'll know what I mean when I say she puts it in the 'vault'. They have a bond that is critical ... and I think all kids need that person.

Mark said: Some days will suck ... just plain be bad days, suck the life out of you - just suck. A great remedy? Get in the car and turn up the music and have a family jam session. Make them listen to music from 'your day' or indulge theirs … in the words of William Congreve, "Music hath charms to soothe the savage breast." #GetTurnt (as the kids say)

Britt said: The tournament circuit … needing to decide if you are going to chase points - points and ranking get you into tournaments. We realized after a few years that, in order to get into bigger tournaments, we had no choice but to chase points in order to continue to move up in the rankings - it is a constant cycle. We played even when it wasn't ideal. Chasing points is a lot like life, you have to work hard to get where you want to go. Most things don't come easy. Best advice here, and it sounds too simple, but focus and take advantage when the opportunities are provided. Cautionary tale as well - DO NOT let your child be defined by their ranking - just like watching a PGA tour event, the 268th ranked person in the world can come in and win an event - the rankings are just a meter used to manage how tournament slots are filled.

Mark said: The tournament director doesn't care if you think it's too windy, rainy, cold or hot to play. They are good at what they do - let them do it.

Britt said: It is still cool to watch the hats coming off and fist bumps when the round is over. Golf is a game of respect, and this is a display of that - I love it.

Mark said: You will have rounds that fly by in 4 hours +/- … and you will have rounds that take 6 hours - and you will think the world has stopped turning. Just like an airline flight, it will end eventually (always have enough snacks on hand).

Britt said: Golf parents and sports parents in general, could really use their own support group - you will run into YOU more often than you realize and that speaks to the importance of a good village (stay tuned, more on that later).

Mark said: Stay out of rulings - have the tournament director's cell phone to get to rules officials. Players should know the simple things but sometimes a situation arises that requires someone with a name badge.

Mark said: Don't go into the woods looking for your kid's ball without another parent there with you - you may be a Sunday School teacher, but people still don't need a reason to doubt you. Err on the side of caution here - it will pay dividends.

Britt said: Pack a bag of everything and have it somewhere in the vehicle. Ibuprofen, bug spray, bandaids, Goody's powders (the orange ones are incredible), CBD oil, Biofreeze, IcyHot, sunscreen, etc. Funny story - at a tournament a dad from another team came from another hole and said a player had a nagging injury and was curious if anyone had KT Tape. 'I do, right here - how much do you need?'

Mark said: Buy a pack of batteries for the rangefinder and put them in the golf bag. It will go dead (but know that if someone in the group has one and yours is dead, they are required to share in most cases).

Britt said: Time heals everything … Sometimes it's hours, sometimes it's days, and sometimes it's years. I've learned that the emotional roller coaster from a variety of scores coming in can make wounds. Those scab covered wounds might bleed again, but eventually there will be a scar there to remind you of the day. My favorite times are when we relive the bad moments on the course and can laugh about them. When we can say what we learned from the bad shots - it's been a great day and time for healing.

Mark said: Pay attention to the SWAG that gets handed out at tournaments - hats, shirts, umbrellas. If you play your cards right (dads) - you will find yourself with some new stuff to wear. 'Oh yeah, son, get the large ... I think the large will fit you well.'

Britt said: Freaky things will happen - Ben broke his toe doing a CrossFit workout two weeks before the start of the 2021 high school tournament season, and we were not sure he would even be able to play at all. With the help of some good cardboard, several doctor friends' advice, and Advil, he powered through it. A teammate ran into back pain the previous year on the way to the state tournament, and a mom from a rival team provided CBD oil to help him finish the rounds. The craziest and funniest (now looking back) is a tournament a few years ago that we played about an hour from home. Ben woke up that morning and came down with a 'crick' in his neck and could not hold his head up straight - It was a Saturday morning so we could not get in to see our chiropractor. We ended up going to see his golf instructor who said 'bring him to me, I can help him'. After doing, I swear, the Mr. Miyagi hand clap and massage - Ben got better. That is, until we got to the course and after riding an hour he had locked up again. We lathered on a whole tube of Icy Hot (we can still smell it in the car after a few years) and plowed ahead.

Mark said: Give a kid grace when he/she makes a simple mistake in his/her counting - trust your gut when they make the same mistake again - pick up on the pattern. As sad as it is, players do try to shave shots - the players in the group have to protect the field by ensuring everyone's score is correct. We've seen some situations get downright ugly, but the math always wins. Britt's dad always said 'if you think you are cheating, you probably are'.

Britt said: To Mark's point above, it is important to let your own player know that integrity is all they have - once they lose it or are doubted, it is gone forever. There are a handful of players that we know have been involved in multiple incidents (remember the pattern above), and we always find ourselves doubting whatever number they post. It's sad, but it's true. That kid will always be the 'one who got caught cheating at xyz tournament' - forgiveness is one thing, but naivety is another.

Mark said: When watching from down the fairway back towards the tee, many times you can watch body language to see where a shot may be landing. We all love seeing when they pick up the tee quickly - that usually means that it is going where intended. Players will learn that hand signals help those, like me, that may be visually challenged get an idea of where to be looking. In our world, a right arm held up and out means that it's 'somewhere' down the right side. A right arm held up with a repeated motion to the right means 'it may be off the planet' to the right.

Britt said: It is OK to tell your kid to 'Double check your score card before you sign it' - once signed, the rules of golf say it is a done deal - if there is an error, it's too late. (Major Championships have been lost over this simple little task)

Mark said: We have a very close friend and fellow golf dad whose only piece of advice to players and parents is DON'T BE TITE with tite pronounced T(eye)T and I am not sure it rhymes with anything - the longest "I" ever in the middle and always, alllwayss said at maximum volume. A kid gets nervous while playing and without fail Rocky says 'HE GOT TITE!!' .... which equates to being nervous and the complete opposite of playing loose.

Britt said: Stay on top of the tournament calendars. Don't forget you are dealing with your child. Go ahead and get a calendar and mark dates that tournaments open for registration. Good advice is to let your child sign up for the tournaments instead of you doing it - make them own it. This way you know the child really wants to play. It takes a lot of courage to give them this responsibility, and I admit we are often micromanagers and try to double check behind Ben to see that he has signed up for what he needs. Mark sometimes signs him up for things not on our regular schedule. Funny sidenote: Just this morning when I drove Ben into the parking lot for the SC Amateur qualifier, he said, 'Mom, where am I and what am I playing in today?'. We both had to find the link. It definitely takes someone staying on top of everything to keep it all straight!

Mark said: Never pull out or WD because it is hard or a horrible day ... that 89 that shows up on your tournament score history tells a story about how hard you worked to overcome adversity. Some days it will feel like the best thing in the world would be just to walk away - but don't, that's where the magic is happening.

Britt said: Pay attention and budget accordingly - tournaments on the road get expensive quickly with hotels, gas, meals, cart rentals, practice round fees, emergency equipment purchases because something got left at home.

Mark said: Play as much as they want to play, not as much as you want them to play.

Britt said: Pull up out of the landing zone (i.e., where tee shots should be landing) when going ahead to spot balls. Golf balls hurt ... and they do not discriminate. I had a bruise on my thigh for weeks from a shot that ended up in the cart with me.

Mark said: Britt pointed this out earlier, but it is worth repeating - always, always, always be respectful of the courses and people you encounter there, it speaks volumes of your child as a player.

Britt said: Meet them as they come off the back of the green with a hug - the same hug for a 72 and you do for a 92. Read this one again ... and don't forget it. I admit I let Mark be the one to go fist pump and hug Ben. I just stand back and watch while my eyes leak most days as he shakes hands with the guys he played with.

Mark said: There will always be someone out there who hits it farther or putts it better - but on a given day ... Any kid can catch lightning in a bottle.

Britt said: Walk when you can - as mentioned earlier, it is therapeutic.

Mark said: Remind and encourage your player to shake the hands of tournament directors and staff after every event and say 'thanks'.

Britt said: Sometimes good shots get bad bounces, sometimes bad shots get good bounces. Golf and life are so similar. It's all in how you deal with the things that happen to you.

Britt said: When it's gonna rain, pack extra everything ... socks, shirts, boxers, shorts and shoes - and towels (use those grungy ones that you never could get yourself to throw away).

Mark said: When they get to experience special things, always have them send a handwritten thank you note. 'When you can do the common things of life in an uncommon way, you will command the attention of the world' - George Washington Carver

Britt said: Some days will be character-building days ... and you will make it to both hands! Our village has their own hand signals that we share across the golf course when we spot each other and one of the most recent is one hand or two hands. We usually don't tell what we are (score for the day) when we meet each other in the fairway ... we give a thumbs up or thumbs down. Those days when we are struggling we might say 'still counting on one hand' - which means we are just five over or better. Those true character-building days are when we make it to two hands for counting. As a mom, look for the good in that day ... find something to focus on other than the score.

Mark said: Make sure they know the rules ... and that you do, too. It may seem like a drop taken anywhere doesn't matter - but you have to protect the field.

Britt said: Hotels ... stay with a group, dinner with the group ... be a part of the village. On the hard days all you want to do is go be alone and sulk. Being with people makes things better. There are always funny stories and the players always seem to bounce back faster when they are around friends. As a parent, you see your child smile after a bad round and you instantly feel better.

Britt said: Don't be that person (that Winona Ride-off-er we will talk more about in a bit) who drives off from greens way too early or comes screeching up to a green while kids are putting. In general, be aware of the surroundings and be respectful. (And oh yeah, that cell phone ringer - the same one that goes off in church ... flip it to silent).

Mark said: Pay attention to the importance of snacking and drinking (for the athlete, not necessarily the parent) - eat and hydrate throughout the round in order to keep up strength and stamina. Avoid sugary snacks and stick with things like beef jerky or protein bars. There is tons of research out there - just google and find a snacking plan that fits your athlete.

Britt said: Know that sometimes there will be NO spectator carts .... That's life, and it sucks sometimes. Our best worst story about this is a course that was 9.5 miles from #1 tee to #18 green (Currahee Club in Toccoa, GA - beautiful, but don't walk it) up and down small mountains in between ... and they let us know that there would be no spectator carts. Remember I mentioned getting good walking shoes?

Mark said: Know that you will pack all of that 'stuff', and they may never use it ... rain gloves, umbrella, extra towels. Teenagers are hard-headed whereas I, I am older and like to maintain a comfortable level of dryness!

Britt said: You will laugh, hurt, cry, get angry, be embarrassed by something you or your child does, be humbled, feel helpless, love harder than you ever have before and feel a pride like no other when your child has their moment.

Britt said: Jot down notes about each round to save for a later date (where, when, what happened, funny stuff, etc.)

Britt said: Keep score cards with stats. Recently, Ben went through a little growing pain and decided he couldn't finish a round. He pulled me into our extra bedroom where I have a hundred score cards and asked me to find a card where he actually finished a good round. He wanted to remember a time when he finished! As we went through the cards he laughed at himself and decided he really had more good days than bad. It wasn't long after that he was able to finish at the state championship. Those cards tell stories that will be remembered forever.

Mark said: Hats off when inside (it's Arnold Palmer's rule)

Britt said: Always keep score for everyone in the group ... at some point, you will need it - don't go waving it like a lawyer ... but have it just in case - it is their responsibility not yours.

Mark said: If you get the opportunity to let your player have a real caddie - do it. Something about watching them interact, make decisions as a team, and learn how to navigate that whole dynamic is awesome (and sometimes you get to keep the bib).

Britt said: Always be looking when someone hits a shot ... a lost ball, for any player in the group, is devastating and they depend on the folks up there watching to see it. Ben recently played in a qualifier with some men in their 30s. I had to walk and would stay ahead to spot balls. The men commented to Ben that his mom sure was good at finding balls and knew exactly where to stand. He told them I followed him around to all his tournaments.

Mark said: To the point above - also know that there are particular times when a player may not want their ball to be found. This will make more sense the more situations you encounter. For the long haulers reading this you are like 'yep, been there and done that.'

Mark said: Know that the rules of golf can feel cruel, and if you sign an incorrect scorecard for a lower score, it is a DQ … and that's not Dairy Queen.

Britt said: Ain't gonna lie, traffic flows smoother after a good day on the golf course … and we have to check ourselves on the bad … perspective - life is easier when things go in our favor. Remember to teach your children that every day isn't perfect, but that every day happens for a reason. Smile and enjoy the days when the putts fall and drives are straight and stay in check when they don't.

Pay Attention

Mark said: You may be thinking you have bought a horror novel if you have made it this far and that is certainly not our intent. We did want to share honestly about those areas in which I/we have made mistakes so you have an opportunity to ensure you don't follow the same path. The journey, though, without a doubt is totally worth it and you will find that, if you pay attention along the way there are memories, laughs, tears of joy, life lessons, encounters, experiences, and relationships created that are absolutely priceless - each and every one. Britt is taking lead on this section which is appropriate given that I am terrible at 'paying attention' in general, and we felt it perhaps a disservice for me to tell anyone anything about the topic. She does pay attention, and it is a blessing.

Britt said: As Mark says above, he is awful at paying attention, but we still love him. One thing I like to point out in particular is about paying attention to the friendships you will create, the relationships that will sprout of a casual conversation, and how much this experience can teach us about life, compassion and being aware and attuned to those we encounter.

If there is one area I would go back and redo it would be the 'Meet the Parents'. One of the golf moms who has given me many tips taught me to put the golfer's name with parents' names beside them in the notes section of my phone. I didn't do that early enough. We spend four hours with someone and think we can remember who they are, but it's hard when you play with so many different children throughout the year. I have to do it because Mark makes up names, and I end up confused trying to remember if the names he gives me are real or not.

Know that the people you meet today you will most likely play with again in the future - and nothing is more embarrassing than someone in the parking lot saying 'Hey, Britt, good to see you', and you cannot remember the name for your life. The names of the players become so familiar, and you always know before the start of the round who you are playing with - so like I mentioned above, once you learn the names of the parents you are with, jot them down in your phone with dates and notes. Further to this point, be nice - you WILL play with the kid again, and you WILL spend another 4-5 hour round with the parents again. Nothing is more awkward than knowing you get to see 'John' today and you just had words with him at the last tournament … it happens - so keep that in mind. One of the most important notes we like to jot down is who brings the best snacks … so that we can be sure to put in a request when we know we are playing together again.

A word here about something I know we do, and I feel like most others do as well (and I would love to know what people call us or at least Mark because I know he has a code name). But, to make it easier to remember people and interactions, we give everyone a code name based on someone they remind us of … we play a lot with 'Robert Wagner' - a dad who is a spitting image of the actor, a kid we call 'little Rickie' because he dresses just like Rickie Fowler (and in turn, his family is simply known as "little Rickie's dad, little Rickie's mom), 'John's ball' (total inside story), 'Henry/George', a gentleman so named because a fellow dad has called him by both - thinking each was correct at the time and now doesn't know which one is, 'Winona Ride-off' who picked up her name because as soon as her son finishes putting, she hits the gas on the cart no matter who she disturbs, and so on and so forth. Many times you will see on my card before I figure out who is who - a kid coded as 'Orange Shirt' or 'Blue Bag' and quite often, that is how we end up referring to them because we may forget their names.

I can usually tell within the first five minutes if the set of parents want to talk or not. I completely respect those who don't want to chit chat and visit during a round of golf because I have days like that as well. Parents need distractions sometimes to take the pressure off the bad moments that might be occurring on the course. One of my favorite days on the course was in 2019 when South Carolina and Georgia were playing football with South Carolina being the underdog. I had service on my phone to watch the game, and a dad playing with us couldn't get his phone to work so he came over to watch as we stopped on each hole and before we knew it, we had no idea what our children were doing. We didn't have a clue of their scores or where they were hitting the ball. We watched Georgia be defeated by an underdog and forgot the game of golf for a few hours. It was a fun day and I remember the instant bond we made.

I also remember the day that we played with a dad and his son whom we had met before and knew they were good folks and the kid was a good player. On this day, though, things were off a bit, and he did not play up to his usual level and his dad - who was normally as wound up as Mark - was as calm as he could be, never said a word at all. Since we had played with them before, we knew something seemed 'off', but we could not put our finger on it and were not dare going to ask. Late in the round as we were coming to the closing holes, the dad shared 'I am just proud (my son) is finishing the round - it has been a tough week. His best friend committed suicide earlier in the week and (my son) was the last person he spoke with before he ended his life, and it has been really hard on him this entire week - thank you guys for letting us enjoy the round with you.' I share because it is important to remember that while a round of golf is happening in that moment, life is happening all around us and it helps if we do pay attention. We never know what families are dealing with in addition to watching a round of golf.

In addition to the story above, a more recent dose of perspective came at a summer SCJGA event at which they gave out red ribbons at check-in to the players. We didn't go to the check-in table so had no idea who the ribbons were meant to commemorate. We asked Ben, and he said 'they told me some man's name that passed away recently, but I don't remember who it was'. So, we pin the ribbon on his hat, and he wears it just like everyone else does and goes on to play the first round with his two playing competitors. After the round we go to dinner with members of the village, and we overhear another one of the kids with us (who also played) mention the name of the gentleman who the ribbons were for - Britt and I quickly put two and two together to realize that they were in honor of a member at the host club who had passed away from a battle with cancer at the age of 44. He had two children, a son and a daughter. You probably guessed it - we had played with that man's son the entire day along with interacting with his wife and had no idea. We were devastated and could not wait to get to her at the start of round two to pass along our condolences. The point being, again, that you never know what someone else has on their plate. Many, many of these children are playing a mental game of golf while dealing with hardship in their lives. Talk to them, let them know they are loved, and try to make everyone feel like they are special. We should be doing that in our lives anyway.

I am a firm believer in God's plans being carried out and that all things happen for a reason. Paying attention to events, details, and interactions is so important. Don't ever think that something happens by mistake ... We have learned, often through disappointments, that right around the corner is a great thing waiting to happen.

In the summer of 2020, Ben didn't qualify for some of the major tournaments on the SCJGA circuit, and I saw his disappointment and had conversations about it not being his turn yet. He didn't want to sit idle, though, so we took the opportunity to sign up for another tournament on the Hurricane Junior Golf Tour that just happened to be hosted at Clemson University (his dad and sister's alma mater). Little did we know how that series of events would play out - he ended up winning the tournament at Clemson (that we never would have been in had he qualified for the SCJGA major) which gave us the opportunity to go play at Disney World in a national tournament.

I say all that not to boast that my son won a tournament - I say that to share that the path allowed us to meet <u>so</u> many people who we now consider friends and have shared so many laughs with - all because he didn't qualify. Trust God's plans in the highs and the lows ... and watch what happens and the people who will cross your path. An interesting footnote is that about a week after we signed up for the Clemson tournament, we found out Ben had made it into the original SCJGA one as well - so we ended up bookended with events, and as I pointed out in **The Carrot and the Stick - What, When and How to Say It** section above, Ben ended up having a tough day - really tough day in the SCJGA event (the one that he had not originally qualified for) to the point that he said 'pull me out of Clemson next week' mid-round. Had I listened to him 'in the moment' and pulled him, we never would have experienced the joys we did from facing adversity head on. Further to this point above and how you have to, as hard as it is, believe in your heart that all things happen for a reason is the story of the 2021 Grant Bennett Invitational in Florence, SC. Ben had never qualified for this event before, so it was a blessing to get to go down and compete against the best golfers in the state when he got accepted in 2021. Day 1 was not his best, but he battled to save the round and keep himself alive to make the cut of top 35. Day 2, he 'found it' and was 1 under par through 14 for the day and well within the cut line - until a triple bogey on the 15th hole meant that a closing birdie on 18 would still leave him 2 shots out of the cut line. He was devastated when he got the news to the point that he just wanted to get in the car and leave - which we did after a period of saying our good-byes. Ben didn't want to speak to anyone. He only told me he wasn't playing anymore. I knew he didn't mean the words he said, and I had to bite my tongue to make sure I didn't say something I didn't need to say.

The wrinkle to this story is this - we had double booked him for the date that would have been the third day of the Grant Bennett. If he made the cut, he would play the final day there - if he missed the cut, he was signed up to play in his first ever SC Amateur qualifier - which in its own right is a pretty cool deal. I asked him about halfway into our 3 hour ride home from Grant Bennett 'do you want to play tomorrow or nah?' and after having some time to cool down from the round and his emotions, he said that he wanted to try it.

In talking with Ben on the drive home about the disappointment of missing the cut, Mark shared with us that his devotion from that morning was James 1:2-4 *2 Consider it pure joy, my brothers and sisters, whenever you face trials of many kinds, 3 because you know that the testing of your faith produces perseverance. 4 Let perseverance finish its work so that you may be mature and complete, not lacking anything* - and that whether he believed it or not, he was supposed to miss the cut because the qualifier held something larger for him. He shot 1 under par in the qualifier meaning he would get to play in his first ever SC Amateur which in and of itself was an amazing learning experience that let me watch Mark caddie for Ben knowing this was a memory they would never forget as a father and a son. Adversity has an awesome way of teaching us lessons and leading us down paths we may never have taken - and introducing us to people we may never have met. Pay attention. Let your children talk about their rounds, but don't take them seriously when they are speaking with heated emotions. Break the tension with a laugh or a threat of a wooden spoon. It gets them every time.

Through all the ups, downs and ins and outs, we have been fortunate to meet a group of golfers and their families who will forever impact our lives. When you hang out in hotels, eat together, struggle on the course together, and cheer each other on from the course, you have no choice but to grow closer. Golf is an individualized sport and the etiquette is different from other sports. You never cheer against another player. You never applaud a bad shot. We have learned you pull just as hard for the children you are playing with as you do for your own. One particular day Ben's friend was having the round of his life. At one point, I didn't even know what Ben's score was because I was watching the amazing shots by his friend. To experience this with other parents is great and moments we don't ever want to forget. If your child isn't the best, it's okay. Be realistic and tell them playing sports is like a mirror of life. He will eventually work with people he doesn't like or people who get on his nerves.

Mark said: Your village is important - get you a village. The interesting thing about villages is that they grow organically, without you really knowing it. I remember when we first moved back to SC from GA in 2016 and Ben participated in his first tournament up here. We met up with one of our really close friends there whose son was also playing - so she was the first in our village. She spoke to at least 10-12 other families and knew kids' names, parents' names … and I recall thinking 'good grief, we don't know a soul and she knows everyone.' The reason is their family had already been playing in the tournaments for a couple of years - and they had met people.

And then one day, years later, it happened - Britt and I brought up that day when we didn't know a soul and remarked at how our village had grown, as if overnight. It happens because you walk the fairways together and become friends - it happens because you become aware of the one who has had a death in the family and you just want to hug them - it happens when you get paired with one of your favorite kids and his grandad brings fresh baked cookies that only grandma 'Nana' can make - it happens when you see their kid struggling and they need you to go comfort them because they can't and vice versa - it happens when you can't get off work to go to a practice round and have to lean on the villagers to do it for you - it happens when the other mom runs into your son while he is looking for money to buy a glove, and she buys it for him and won't let you pay her back because he is partly hers - it happens when they all play bad and you get to sit around the pool at the beach and talk about much better tomorrow will be, even if it doesn't end up that way - it happens when you watch one of your 'other' kids shoot the round of his life and you get so excited that you hug and kiss him on the television cameras (before his parents can even make it to him) and the news crew says 'the first person to greet him after his 62 was his dad' (lots of jokes after that one - but it is a memory we will never forget).

It happens when you find yourself telling your 'other kids' to tuck their shirts in, take their hats off, shake hands when they meet people - it happens when you find a dead snake and put it on the shoulder of a fellow villager just to watch the reaction - it happens when you laugh so hard that you wake up sore the next morning - it happens when you are so sticky dirty that you all make the decision to go to the same restaurant so that no one will talk about how bad you smell alone - it happens when you watch one of your 'other' kids miss a putt that meant something, and it breaks your heart as much as their parents' - it happens when you know you can trust your own with any member of the village and know that you could leave them there 6 months and they would never miss a beat - it means not trading money but trading children - it happens when you have a whole lotta options for good cop, bad cop - it happens when everyone in the village knows everything so no one can get away with anything - it happens when you get to see new found friends when you visit certain courses and tournaments - it happens when you can look across opposite fairways and see people from your village and through an elaborate set of hand signals know who's mad, who's happy and who is in need of shock therapy - it happens when you get text messages during the round from villagers not even there asking how things are going - it happens when you have a support team of instructors and equipment folks that will drop everything they are doing for the village - it happens when you get so excited to play with certain families because you know you'll focus on everything but golf.

It happens while watching other mamas and daddies crying with joy when your child achieves something, and in sadness when they don't - it happens when you watch a grandad so filled with faith he is about to burst into praying over your village children as they hit the road to go play - it happens when a surprise rainstorm comes up and you get to dig into someone else's car for gear (no underwear, though … the village does not include that provision) - and lastly, it happens when you find out one of the village dads is so sick with COVID that he is afraid he is taking his last breath and it takes him months to get back to the course and when he does, and you see him, he runs to get to you and you to him - and you hug like you've been family forever and he says 'I love you man' and you say 'I love you, too brother' … it happens.   Build your village.

In writing about the Village above, it brings to mind this inspirational story below and is a great reminder that we should be aware, thankful and share our appreciation for those in our village:

SHOWING APPRECIATION: WHO'S PACKING YOUR PARACHUTE?
AUTHOR UNKNOWN

Charles Plumb was a US Navy jet pilot in Vietnam. After 75 combat missions, his plane was destroyed by a surface-to-air missile. Plumb ejected and parachuted into enemy hands. He was captured and spent 6 years in a communist Vietnamese prison. He survived the ordeal and now lectures on lessons learned from that experience!

One day, when Plumb and his wife were sitting in a restaurant, a man at another table came up and said, "You're Plumb! You flew jet fighters in Vietnam from the aircraft carrier Kitty Hawk. You were shot down!"

"How in the world did you know that?" asked Plumb.

"I packed your parachute," the man replied. Plumb gasped in surprise and gratitude. The man pumped his hand and said, "I guess it worked!" Plumb assured him, "It sure did. If your chute hadn't worked, I wouldn't be here today."

Plumb couldn't sleep that night, thinking about that man. Plumb says, "I kept wondering what he had looked like in a Navy uniform: a white hat; a bib in the back; and bell-bottom trousers. I wonder how many times I might have seen him and not even said 'Good morning, how are you?' or anything because, you see, I was a fighter pilot and he was just a sailor." Plumb thought of the many hours the sailor had spent at a long wooden table in the bowels of the ship, carefully weaving the shrouds and folding the silks of each chute, holding in his hands each time the fate of someone he didn't know.

Now, Plumb asks his audience, "Who's packing your parachute?" Everyone has someone who provides what they need to make it through the day.

A couple of closing notes about the people you will meet: You will play with 'that kid' and 'those parents' from time to time. The key is to never be 'that kid' or 'those parents' that people cringe at when they see that they are paired with you. Choose kindness, always.

Parenting styles differ - we don't raise theirs, they don't raise ours (except in the village - in the village, we all raise everyone). Otherwise, it is not our job to provide our opinion to someone else about how they raise or manage their child(ren). Just as we would not expect anyone to come tell us how to do our job with ours. Stay in your lane

… unless someone drives into yours, and if they do, choose kindness until you can't.

This Really Happened: Short Stories from the Rough

'Anything that hurts you can teach you, and if it keeps hurting you, it's because you haven't learned the lesson.'

−UNKNOWN

Britt said: These stories, sadly, tragically, or comically, really happened to us, and I am sure that by the time we are done traveling, we will have enough to fill a complete book. Hold onto the stories you create - they are what build memories (even though some, we'd rather forget).

The Ice Chest & The Dollar General

Mark said: We have come to be very close friends with a fellow golf dad who recently recalled this story for us as we were talking about some of the mistakes we've made along the way. I'll call him Joe, here, to protect his identity - but if you ever meet Joe, you're gonna share a laugh - he's just that funny. Joe shared this story as one of his un-finest moments. Years ago, Joe's son was beginning to show signs of promise on the golf course - breaking 80 every now and then, but not yet a regular occurrence, and certainly not in competition. The son played the front 9 at a local course and was a couple over par at the turn and the dad admits 'I let myself think, today is the day - we are about to shoot a mid 70 round.' Now the back nine of this course is brutal …. with a particularly rough gauntlet on holes 13-17 … and it happened. 2 over on the front quickly ballooned to '10 or 12 over on the backside' to hear Joe tell it.

Joe is mad … not mad at his son, but at the missed opportunity *(he now admits that he had NO Idea how hard the backside was until he had the chance to see it more and more).* They throw the clubs in the SUV and head out - all the while Joe telling his son they are quitting golf and taking up badminton - as they left the parking lot, he fishtailed a little and he just 'drove mad' to get home as quickly as possible. It wasn't long until he noticed he had driven so hard the ice chest in the back had turned over, so he whipped into a Dollar General to fix it. When he opened the hatch on the vehicle, the ice chest poured into the parking lot and went everywhere … a complete mess. Joe said that a lady, who was parked beside him, was in the process of backing out and just sat there and stared at him … and Joe stared back and yelled "WHAAATTTTT??" at the top of his lungs. What Joe did not know at the time was that the lady had made eye contact with the son sitting in the passenger seat - and he was slowly shaking his head mouthing 'I'm sorrrrrrrrrry'.

I realize without knowing these guys, you may think Joe is crazy, and he would let you know in that moment, he probably had gone a little nuts. We laugh now at the visual of this busted ice chest strewn across the parking lot while this random lady is trying to take it all in and figure out what in the heck has just happened. She had no idea the tension the moment held … and how looking back now, it is a learning moment for us all. The best part about our village growing is Joe gets to tell the story over and over as more and more people join us - and it gets funnier every time we ask him to share it.

Could I Use Your Restroom?

Britt said: Ben may have been in the 8th grade when this story transpired - we were playing in a high school team tournament at a super nice course with gargantuan houses that I swear could have fit three of my houses inside one of them. Super nice landscaping, super nice cars - you felt like you needed to stand up a little straighter and make sure your shirt was tucked in just to stand around and watch golf. Spectators were not allowed to have carts - only the coach.

With that as a backdrop for context, we have a dad on our team who is the one who 'it' always happens to. Everyone has that guy in the group, and for us it was - let's call him 'Chip'. Well, Chip had made a few comments throughout the morning that his coffee had kicked in *(which all southerners will understand)* and he was getting close to an emergency situation. We were at a spot on the course with no bathrooms around at all … and his only saving grace was going to be if his wife called the coach to come pick him up on the golf cart (all parents were walking along with the kids). She did and thought she had solved the issue … everyone separated as the hole was being played - some go up, some stay back to watch from different vantage points. A while later the golf coach comes riding by on the cart and asks Chip's wife where he is - Coach has been looking for him to 'rescue' him, but he is nowhere to be found - like he has disappeared. We did not learn until later that Chip hit absolute 9-1-1 status and knew that he was not going to make it all the way back to the clubhouse on a cart. So, without telling anyone, he chose a yard that was adjacent to the tee box he had been at and climbed the winding hill to their deck and eventually to the door - where he rang the bell and asked awkwardly 'would it be at all possible for me to use your restroom?'. And he did.

Yes, he did. He said he stayed there for a while and was even kind enough to spray a little poo-pourri spray on his way out.

'I Guess Maybe He Did Know the Rule, Then'

Mark said: Another fellow golf dad who we will call 'Ricky' was following his son at a very prestigious high school tournament with a field from across the country - a lot of talented players and an opportunity to play against people who we have never met before. Britt and I were a group ahead, and we always keep tabs on each other as the day goes by - so we can usually tell when someone ahead or behind us is in trouble, looking for a ball, etc.

I notice that Ricky's son is walking towards the trees and area marked as a hazard on a short par 4 that we had just played, and it is obvious that he doesn't immediately see his ball - meaning it is likely in the hazard. Ricky, in an effort to help locate the ball (which he and most parents, including us, do all day long for their own kid and others) walks over to the area where his son is searching and encounters another gentleman who happened to be in that area as well (turns out, his son is playing in another group, but he is hanging back and watching other players on the team). So this gentleman declares pretty early that it is obvious that the ball is in the hazard and that Ricky's son has two options available (given the layout and scenario). Ricky is a little struck that this guy is so quick to offer the ruling AND to call off the search - so he lets him know in a kind but firm tone, 'hey boss, we still have time to search for the ball and go through the options'. The gentleman repeats - these are the only two options he has (and proceeds to share what they are) ... and this gets under Ricky's skin a little, because he wants to evaluate a third option. At this point, Ricky shares with the gentleman, this time in a more direct and firm tone

'I said, we GOT IT BOSS!' Tensions are high, and the son eventually takes the drop (using one of the two options that were presented).

The day goes on and as often happens, Ricky forgets about the incident until he is talking with another dad from the same team that this other gentleman was supporting. This dad is pointing out people across different holes that are there supporting their team - and he says, 'and you may know that guy up there … he's a big supporter of our team' to which Ricky says "never met him, who is it?" (*Ricky didn't offer up that he had JUST been in an argument with the same person being pointed out hours earlier*). 'That's XYZ (name omitted on purpose), he played on the PGA Tour and his son plays on our team.'

And Ricky said to himself 'I guess maybe he did know the rule, then'.

A Little Nod Will Do Ya

Mark said: There is a story shared by a golf dad about the time he was watching a group of kids, none of which were his own, play the final holes of a tournament. There was a young man playing who had never seen the course before and was learning the layout as he went. He got to the 16th hole which is a short, short par 4 with trouble lurking long and on either side. For someone who has never played the course, it 'looks' like you should just take the driver and blow it down as far as you can - but the locals know, the percentage play is to lay back.

The players are all on the tee box jotting down scores from the prior hole and making decisions about the shot they want to play off the tee. This kid, who we will call Wally, is confused and really grinding over this decision. And this dad shares that he watched as Wally puts his hand on his driver and begins to pull it up and out of the bag in slow motion and while doing so just happened to make eye contact with him. The dad doesn't say a word but just slowly shakes his head from left to right in a 'not a good idea' motion, and the kid, again in slow motion slides the driver back down in the bag and moves his hand over several clubs before landing on a hybrid and, again, in slow motion, begins pulling it up out of the bag, making eye contact with this dad who is now shaking his head in the up-down direction. What makes this funny is that these two people are not related but this dad could see the total confusion on Wally's face. A word of warning - tell your player to be careful about taking advice from others - this dad was being nice, but it could have ended badly.

'If You Hadn't Had Them Three Bogeys'

Mark said: Ben had the opportunity to play in a tournament at Disney World in 2020 with kids from all over the country and some international. On the second day, we got paired with a young man whose family could have been our own - it was like a reunion with family members we had never met, and we were laughing and cutting up within 3 minutes of meeting each other.

Ben comes out of the gate hot … and gets it to 3 under par through 6 holes on a difficult golf course, and then as we get to 7, 8 and 9 - he bogeys each of them to fall back to even at the turn. He is running 'hotter than a two dollar pistol' as George Jones put it, and I knew I was not allowed to talk to him so I told my new buddy, the dad of a playing competitor, 'hey, I can't speak to Ben but it'd be great if someone was able to let him know it's gonna be ok', - and I thought maybe he'd say - 'hey, keep it up', 'finish strong', or something to that effect. As Ben walked past him he said 'Hey Ben, just so you know … if you hadn't had them three bogeys you'd be three under par right now.' (Ben, had no idea the personality this guy had because he had not gotten to interact with him like we had so it made it that much funnier). Needless to say - it broke the tension and Ben proceeded to birdie the next 3 holes and get BACK to 3 under par for the day and really climb the leaderboard.

And then it happened - a really tough par 4 that had trouble everywhere, and Ben found the hazard off of the tee and was left with a shot of over 200 yards over water off of a skinny lie after already taking a penalty drop. I was standing up near the cross point of the water line with this other dad, and we watched Ben playing his third shot. He hit it, and we knew he didn't catch it all, and it landed in the water - sploosh. This dad looks over at me and said 'Well, he just %&*#ing BLOWED it right there! … one swing and the whole day is undone.' Ben made triple, so is back to even par for the day after being 3 under two separate times and is now REALLY running hot under the collar.

No one dared speak to him as he just needed to get the anger out so we all migrated to the next green and waited for the boys to come up. Ben is still obviously shaken up and I tell the guy again, 'man, I wish I had the words to say right now', and he said 'I got it, don't you worry'. I thought that this time something purely poetic was going to emerge from his lips.

'Hey Ben … if you hadn't had that triple back there …. You'd be 3 under, AGAIN!' and Ben smiled and came back down to earth.

I share that story for a couple of reasons - one is to further emphasize the joy you will get out of the people you meet on the course, and secondly, to reiterate what was said earlier about sometimes the voice they need to hear is not yours - it can make all the difference.

Cracker Barrel Story

Mark said: Apparently, this story is so funny to Britt it's gonna get it's own Mark said/Britt said - I'll go first. One of my biggest regrets as a golf dad will also live forever as one of my family's stories they love to use to needle me with at random times. And while on the surface it brings about some giggles (amongst them), it still makes me think about who I was in those moments that day … and why I wish someone had told me 'there are gonna be days like this, and you are going to have to be prepared to handle them'. We are confident as well that after reading this story, you will have some insight into why we settled on the final title for this book because *this* **drive home was the one that sparked the idea that you now hold in your hands.**

The story, which now lives on in the McKinney family lore, is simple, yet profound. Ben was entering day two of one of the SCJGA Majors at a course that is known to eat your lunch if you aren't hitting it well. He had played very well on day one and was in the next to last group going out on day 2 playing with much older and much more experienced kids – and the nerves were apparent. Long story short, every out of bounds stake that we didn't notice on day 1 became like a magnet on day 2 – it was hot, he 'beat it' and my frustration got the better of me – I think it was more disappointment for him knowing what was at stake had he kept it together (additional exemptions, points, etc). I cannot even remember what Britt, my wife, asked me after the round, but I replied with some short, hot-tempered response because I was looking for something to be mad at.

We left the course in silence, drove to a Cracker Barrel for lunch (which I ate in silence), and then I drove home on I-85 like a mad man because I was so angry. To hear my family tell it, they say we were going 'a hundred and no one could talk' … which is an exaggeration … for the most part.

Britt said: I LOVE THIS STORY! My version of the drive down I-85 going 95 is a little different than Mark's. Some background - My mama and daddy hardly ever said a kind word to each other. I grew up in a house where 'cutting' each other down was part of life. Don't feel bad for me, it made me tough. Having two older brothers who constantly picked on me and parents who made smart comments to each other often led me to having a personality trait that allows me to make uncomfortable situations funny. Daddy was the best at it - I learned it from him. He would come in from the golf course with stinky socks, sweaty clothes, smelling like a Marlboro, and Mama would start blessing him out for dirtying up the house she had just spent all day cleaning. While this would have made others uncomfortable to hear them go back and forth, he would break the tension by saying, 'Ain't she cute when she is mad!' And then life would go on as normal.

On this particular day, Ben couldn't have played any worse if he had tried. It was awful. He looked completely different than the child who had been perfect the day before. As we walked around the course and watched him, I watched Mark completely change his demeanor. He was popping his knuckles, mumbling to himself, and typing notes in his phone. I told him to settle down and he jumped all over me. My initial reaction was to run over him with the golf cart, but I wasn't sure that would make things any better. On the 17th green I had had enough and told him to either look like he was enjoying the round or go to the car. He started power walking toward the 18th tee box and never stopped. At this point, I was frustrated too! I haven't said this before, but I am a Mama Bear. I can talk about my children all day long, but NO ONE, including their father, better utter something ugly about them. To say there was tension in the car was an understatement. Add to it hot weather and a set of friends who wanted to go out to eat after the horrible round - this was a time I considered Ubering home from the course.

We followed our friends to go eat, and Mark never uttered a word during the meal except what he wanted from the menu. It was awful. When we got back in the car and started down I-85 I knew I had to do something and being like my daddy, I felt I had to break the tension. Mark didn't think it was funny, but it gave the children the opportunity and permission to speak again because everyone in the car was afraid to say a word. I announced to the car, 'Children, I want you to remember this day forever. I want you to look around and see what is going on. This is the day where your daddy is driving 95 going down I-85 because he is mad.' Mark's hands gripped the steering wheel even harder, but the children and I laughed until we almost cried. We joke on the side without Mark knowing that we hope it isn't going to be a '95 going down I-85' kind of day.

Mark is right - he was mad that day. If I could give you advice, I'd say everyone can't be mad. Someone has to break the tension and be like my daddy who would immediately have said - 'Let that $#^! Go!'

What Did I Hit?

Britt said: This story is less than a week old as I write this, so is still fresh enough that the ones who know about it are still just laughing randomly when they are reminded of it. Mark and I were standing on the edge of the first fairway waiting on Ben to hit into the green and noticed some villagers who were playing into the green on #5, which basically runs adjacent to #1. We look across the way and notice the dad is laughing so hard he can barely control it, and it is obvious that he's going to make his way over to us to share what in the world has him so riled up. Turns out that his son had hit a tee ball into a tree off of #5 tee box and it ricocheted almost behind him. Being down the fairway waiting on the tee shot to land, the dad was confused when it didn't, but quickly got word from some other parents on what had transpired. He makes the trek back up towards the tee box to offer a hand in case they had trouble finding it. By the time he got back it was located, so he did <u>another</u> u turn and headed back down the fairway and past this group of players and parents that he had <u>just</u> come by but had not seen the first time. So, as he is driving by this mass of people he is noticing who all it is, saying hello, waving - all the while continuing to drive ahead without looking. He still had his head turned when he said he felt like the bottom of the golf cart 'fell out' and he knew he had hit something - but was too embarrassed to stop and check. He went on a little more before finally stopping and realizing that he had run over a humongous turtle and was quick to say he saw him reemerge from his shell, safe and alert. A lady sitting nearby who was helping spot tee shots told him 'that poor guy has been working so hard all day to get across the fairway and you hit him'.

The Truth is All We Have Son

Mark said: As was mentioned before, if a child <u>ever</u> gets a reputation as a cheater - it <u>never</u> goes away. A couple of summers ago, there was a player, let's call him 'Jerry', who had been involved in a few blatant instances of miscounting his score when it came time to check in at the scoring tent. So much so that parents who were paired with him were on high alert all day - to ensure the field was protected against any wrongdoing. The next tournament comes along, and we see Jerry is paired with some very good friends of ours and their son, so we immediately reach out to, let's call him 'Larry', the dad, and say 'hey, just a reminder to be on alert today because the kid you all are playing with has been questioned several times over his score'. And that, in and of itself, was like putting Matlock on the case *(if you are too young to know who Matlock is, go ahead and Google it ... we will wait).*

There were a couple of things that happened in-round - one instance of Jerry claiming his ball was not out of bounds - but the best was the swing and miss that would transpire late in the day. Larry had been across the fairway helping his son locate an errant tee shot when he spotted Jerry on the opposite side, in the trees and bushes - so he hightailed it across to watch it all unfold. Jerry's ball is right up against a high piece of grass making it nearly impossible to get a club on the ball to advance it. He tries it though, and his swing misses everything - whiffed it. Being determined, though, Jerry hammers down on it again and this time advances the ball down the fairway and as he walks out of the woods says to Larry, 'That was a good practice swing on that first one.'

Larry (aka Matlock) drives closer to Jerry as they are now making their way down the fairway and says 'Son, did you mean to hit that ball the first time?' to which Jerry replies, 'No, sir, it was a practice swing.'

Larry gives him one more opportunity and drives closer, lowers his sunglasses to the bridge of his nose so that he can 'look him in the eye' as he puts it, and says 'Son, are you sure?' to which Jerry says. 'Well, to tell the truth, yes, I meant to hit it on the first swing', and Larry replied, 'The truth is all we have son.' (which has become a common refrain anytime we see Larry now). To add to the drama of the day, when Jerry got to the scoring tent, he still tried to get away with a few strokes he had miscounted but everyone was on high alert and he didn't get away with it.

Advice from People Who Know

'Experience is what you get when you don't get what you want.'

−David Feherty at 2021 US Open Championship

Britt said: We are fortunate to have an amazing circle of friends & friends of friends, and as we alluded to earlier, a great village. To that point, we have asked two questions of each of the individuals listed below to garner feedback, advice and guidance from their perspectives - all of which are relevant, credible, and well respected. We have posed these questions within the context of a 'junior athlete' because we feel like the responses can and will span all sports. Many of the respondents are, by nature of our circle and the focus of this book, golf-centric but we have found that the principles learned and taught are many times, sport agnostic - because it is about the child, the player and their relationship with us, the parent.

We offer our collective (Mark said and Britt said) voices of thanks to each of the individuals below who were so gracious with their time, their friendship, and their feedback. This is an immensely diverse group of backgrounds, experiences and perspectives, and we are blessed to be able to share them with you all. Their words are personal, powerful, and have the potential to have a lasting impact - enjoy!

The two questions we posed are as follow:

1. How can parents most effectively support their child(ren) as a junior athlete(s)?
2. What is one piece of advice you have for a junior athlete?

Dabo Swinney: Head Football Coach, Clemson University

How can parents most effectively support their child(ren) as a junior athlete(s)? Just support them and love them. Let the coach be the critical one and you be the parent. Help them navigate the success and failure and teach them to enjoy the journey.

What is one piece of advice you have for a junior athlete? Don't let the focus be on being THE best ... The focus should always be on being YOUR best. Can't get All In results with half in effort ... gotta put the work in and love the grind. There is no shine without the grind. Also ... enjoy the journey and have fun.

Ryan Dailey, PGA: Co-Founder of Operation 36 Golf, 2013 Carolinas PGA Youth Player Development Award, 2018 & 2019 GRAA Top 50 Growth of the Game Teaching Professional, 2019 & 2020 Golf Digest Best Teacher in NC. Instagram @ryandaileygolf, on the web at op36. golf/ and YouTube at Operation 36 Golf.

Operation 36 Golf was started in 2010 by Ryan and Matt Reagan to increase family participation at the golf course. With no idea what they were doing, they tried every program that was available at the time to no avail. After 5 years, they were stuck and couldn't figure out why so many players were quitting the game. They switched gears and instead of focusing all of their energy on games and activities to run on the putting green and driving range...they put the majority of their energy into how to get players on the golf course and falling in love with playing the game. The Operation 36 on-course development model was founded and participation skyrocketed. Coaches from around the world started contacting them to learn and then use the program at their facilities. An iOS and Android app were built to supplement the training from the Coach and help a Coach organize their Academy. Currently, Operation 36 Adult and Junior programming specifically designed for beginner golfers are offered at over 600 locations in over 15 countries around the world.

How can parents most effectively support their child(ren) as a junior athlete(s)? Show you CARE by your actions, not just your words.

I get it, it's hard. We are all juggling schedules with work and thousands of other things. However, if it's important enough to you, you'll do it, if not, you'll make an excuse. After observing parents for years as an athlete myself in multiple sports and now for the last 15+ years coaching/parenting in golf, baseball, softball, soccer, gymnastics, karate, basketball, and scootering it seems like the most effective parents show they CARE by their actions. It isn't just the words that are spoken.

The child then perceives, "Dad cares about me, he spends time with me."

5 core actions that I have observed parents do over the years to show they CARE:

- Attending a child's event or training as often as possible. Physically being present matters.
- Playing catch in the backyard (or insert any other sport) on a consistent basis.
- Dedicating a specific day and time each week to take their child to the ball field, golf course or gym to get in some extra training.

- After an event, give them a big hug (or when they are older, put your arm around them) and tell them, "I love to watch you play, my favorite part of the week is being able to watch you play."
- Hand-writing a note to their child after a tough game, match, or competition that states how proud you are of them and that you believe in them.

These are all actions that show you CARE. That would be my recommendation to parents. Again, I get it. It's not easy, if it was easy everyone would do it.

What is one piece of advice you have for a junior athlete? Anything worthwhile takes time. All of us are beginners when we start. We all shot 120 before we shot 100 before we shot 80 before we shot 65. We've all made plenty of quadruple bogeys, lost hundreds of golf balls, and made plenty of swings when we started out where we looked down and the ball didn't move…lol.

It takes time. If you are just starting out, it is a marathon, not a sprint. Can you stick with it long enough, to acquire the skills to get good enough to reach your goals? As we are finding by observing golfers over the last 13 years with Operation 36, talent has very little to do with success. Success is just a matter of getting your reps in overtime. Some are willing to make the sacrifice, get the reps in (playing and training) and some give up before they have a chance to acquire the skills necessary to reach their goals.

The most successful players we have been around fall in love with the improvement process. They view this process almost like a scientist doing an experiment. Each day they go play and train, they learn something new that will make them 1% better. They jot that note down in a journal and do the same thing the next day. After 3-5 years of doing that, they have improved a lot. When they have bad days, they know it is part of the process of improvement, they jot down the notes from that day in their journal and they can't wait for the next day to come to try it again. They know the longer the process the more of an advantage it is to them as they will have figured out plenty of ways that don't work (unintended outcomes) along with plenty of formulas that put them in the best position to succeed.

Anything worthwhile takes time.

Justin Fleming: South Carolina Junior Golf Association (SCJGA) Senior Director: Originally hired in 2002 as a Tournament Assistant, promoted to Director of Youth Development in 2006 and became heavily involved in the Clubs for Kids, Golf in Schools and Chapter Program. Justin now serves as the Senior Director where he oversees the various developmental programs as well as all SCJGA Major Competitions.

How can parents most effectively support their child(ren) as a junior athlete(s)? I think the best way a parent can support their junior athlete is by being their biggest cheerleader and giving them unconditional love and support. I can't tell you how many times I hear junior golfers complain during scoring about how angry their parents get when they fail, hit a bad shot, or shoot a high score. Not to mention me witnessing parents show their emotions on their sleeves in the middle of a tournament when your junior is playing bad. Your junior golfer is not trying to play badly, hit a bad shot or get nervous but that's part of growing and learning this game. The moment they begin fearing your response to their failures you've added another layer of difficulty to this already difficult game.

What is one piece of advice you have for a junior athlete? Figure out the best balance for grinding and really working hard on your game and taking plenty of breaks. You really need balance to make sure and keep your sport fresh. That might mean multiple sports for some, taking breaks for others and finding other hobbies and interests. Ben Hogan was quoted as saying "every day I miss practicing takes me one day longer to get better." While this is very true for some people, I think it's equally important to not be afraid or feel guilty for taking time off every now and again. The last thing you want to do as a junior athlete is turn your sport into a job.

Scott McNealy: co-Founder and former CEO of Sun Microsystems, Founder of Curriki.org, father of PGA Tour Professional Maverick McNealy.

How can parents most effectively support their child(ren) as a junior athlete(s)?

- Live for your children, not through them.
- Don't yell at the referees.
- Travel with your child on overnight games or tournaments. Do not delegate raising your child.
- When your child has a complaint about the coach, tell them to go talk to the coach themselves. It is fine if you sit in and listen, but just observe and discuss the meeting alone with your child after.
- Our rule was get straight A's or you were not eligible for sports.

- Do your homework before you are allowed to go play or practice. Sports are a treat and reward, not a chore.
- We never demanded that they do extra practice. It had to be their decision.
- Tell your child that if the drugs don't kill them, you will.
- If you pay to have your child play, tell the coach you expect equal time during games. If your child is paid to play, don't expect equal time during games. School sports are not pay to play, don't expect equal time.
- Keep your house a safe house with respect to food. Eliminate junk food, sugar, etc. Food is fuel for an athlete. Work with them on nutrition. Set a great example with how the entire family eats, and don't be fat and out of shape. Be a role model.
- Congratulate their efforts, not the result.
- Five parts praise, one part constructive feedback. Never "criticize", only offer suggestions.
- Come down hard on lost tempers, foul mouths, disrespect of adults.

What is one piece of advice you have for a junior athlete?

- If you are not enjoying it, don't do it. It's your call.
- Work harder than anyone else on the team.
- Protect and support the weaker athletes from any bullies on the team.

Susan McNealy: Mother of PGA Tour Professional Maverick McNealy who concurs with husband Scott's thoughts above and offers these additional thoughts.

How can parents most effectively support their child(ren) as a junior athlete(s)?

- Praise a good attitude and effort - not results. Work hard, don't complain.
- Make them responsible for packing all gear and arriving at practices and games on time.

What is one piece of advice you have for a junior athlete

- Get enough sleep! We didn't let our boys do sleepovers. No phones, computers or tvs in bedroom.
- Have blood work done by a doctor and analyzed to see what supplements are needed. For example, Vitamin D made a big difference with our boys.
- Find a mentor. Maverick, while a freshman at Stanford, learned all he could from Patrick Rodgers, star senior on the golf team.
- Read! Personal favorite is Golf from Point A by Susie Meyers. It can be applied to all sports and life.

Matt Krug, PhD: Matt is a licensed psychologist serving as the Director of Psychological Services for the Milwaukee Brewers Baseball team for 10 years. An active member for advocacy and professional standards and policies in MLB, he has presented multiple times to MLB and MLBPA on standards of care and structure of Psychology departments in baseball. He oversees and implements programs designed to increase performance and treat the mental health of the players. While his focus is on the major league team, he is also involved in development through the minor league system as well as player selection.

He holds an MA in Sport Psychology from San Diego State University, an MA in Counseling from Marquette University and a PhD from Marquette University in Counseling Psychology. He was a three sport Division 3 athlete and All Star in the Northwoods Collegiate Wooden Bat League. Since 2000, he has served as President of the Midwest Institute of Performance, LLC. Consulting experience includes IMG Academies in Florida, NCAA rowing, NCAA basketball, NCAA golf, individual PGA TOUR players, and NFL athletes. He is also a certified consultant for the NBA.

How can parents most effectively support their child(ren) as a junior athlete(s)? / What is one piece of advice you have for a junior athlete?

There is a ton of data around performance (i.e., greens hit, strokes gained, putts per round, etc.) but nothing hard and fast around psychology and the different dynamics (i.e., little Johnny's daddy was at 90% of golf matches and he was successful versus scenario B where Sally's dad was only at 10% of matches)

My main 3 points are as follows and can be supported with research:

1. Long term focus
2. Attachment/attachments
3. Don't have singular path focus

    a. Parents must have a long-term focus … not short term. Too much is based on short-term decisions (i.e., should we even go to the next tournament given that we just rinsed two in the water knowing the impact that can have?). Parents must know that this is a long-term thing … with baseball it can be years of outlook and in golf, it must be at least several months … versus the tweak now, immediate results expectation.

    b. <u>Attachment</u> - Psychology research exists around how a family is structured and how a secure attachment is formed - the relationship. I see it in the school research … 'nuclear families of mom, dad, kids' provide one model but if there is a single parent home and then the attachment shifts to the teacher having to take on some of that burden/responsibility, it can get wonky. If I have a 25-year-old in front of me who has signed for $2 million, and his dad was there for the whole journey … but now the dad is not there anymore - sometimes it is because the child is 'tired' of his dad being there because the sport was the only attachment. There must be <u>more attachment than just the sport - there must be a deeper relationship</u> - else we run the risk of damaging, destroying or at a minimum, adversely impacting family relationships.

    <u>Attachments</u> - A young athlete will soon realize what all is attached to the outcomes (the <u>attachments</u> versus the

relationship <u>attachment</u> above) … 'my parents spent all this money to get me a scholarship, so I have to perform well and if I don't, I risk not achieving their goal' … that is hard on kids. I would have a long-term approach and then focus on how you are developing the attachment with your child … and when and where are they learning what is <u>attached to their performance?</u> Many times, the model of college scholarship is used to justify the pushing of the child when in theory, instead of paying $40K for all the training and such … could have just paid the tuition. There is lots of pressure on kids dealing with the <u>attachments</u> once they are aware of them … not many kids, even older or adults, could deal with that pressure.

c. Multiple Paths - I will walk into the baseball clubhouse today and see draft picks … ½ that were on someone's radar at 16 and ½ are from nowhere … Parents think - I have to get my kid in at 12 or I am losing ground when in fact, there are lots of different ways to get there … lots of paths … so many different paths … don't focus on the ONE way to get to where you want your kid to go … many parents get the kid in at 12 and he/she is burned out at 18 … other parents see a kid hop in at 18 and thrive.

Dr. Mark Broadie: Mark Broadie is the Carson Family Professor of Business at Columbia Business School. Professor Broadie's research addresses issues in quantitative finance and sports analytics and, more generally, methods for decision making under uncertainty. He currently teaches courses on business analytics and sports analytics. In his golf research, Broadie developed the strokes gained stats that are used by the PGA Tour. He works with a number of PGA Tour pros and writes a monthly column for GOLF magazine. His New York Times bestselling book Every Shot Counts uses data and analytics to measure and improve golf performance and strategy. Broadie worked with Turner Sports to bring the first live golf win probabilities to the network broadcast of the Woods-Mickelson match. He has been a member of the USGA's handicap research team since 2003. He developed the Golfmetrics app to allow amateur golfers to better analyze their golf games. Professor Broadie received a BS from Cornell University and a PhD from Stanford University.

How can parents most effectively support their child(ren) as a junior athlete(s)? I'd encourage young children not to specialize in any one sport too early in order to develop a range of physical abilities. Don't pressure children about results. Focus instead on improving each year.

What is one piece of advice you have for a junior athlete? To put in the needed time to become an expert, you need to love the sport, so have fun!

Chris Hodge: PGA Teaching Professional, played college golf at The Citadel.

How can parents most effectively support their child(ren) as a junior athlete(s)? Managing kids and their athletic pursuits is so different from kid to kid and parent to parent. Knowing what motivates them, how they are organized, what makes them happy, how they deal with adversity and supporting them comes in different packages. My key points for parents and how they can support:

- Money so they can afford to have the right equipment, uniforms, instruction and transportation.
- Encouraging them to go play, practice, work on their physical fitness and eating habits.
- Reminding them that it is fun for them not a job.
- Helping them learn how to set goals - small ones that they reach (goals set too high are useless) that lead into achieving the larger goals.
- Helping them learn how to find the bounce back - overcoming adversity and disappointment.
- Know your child and then surround them with people that overcome your weakness as well as the student - you cannot be everything for them.
- With all of this - it still ultimately depends on the kid - do they want it, love it and are they willing to make the sacrifices to do the work and enjoy the ride?

What is one piece of advice you have for a junior athlete?

- Enjoy the journey knowing there will be ups and downs. With all athletic adventures - you can become the biggest fish in your pond - then you go to the next bigger pond with all the other biggest fish. You become the biggest fish there and go to another bigger pond which is a lake of the biggest of the biggest and the process keeps going.
- It is hard to feel that you belong and just focus on achieving your goals, working on all the things that got you there. Be accepting of changing the process if there is something better for you or if you find a better way - learn from all the people around you.

- Decide if you love the game enough to do the work, make goals, enjoy the ups and downs of the journey. If not - then accept you may not be the best and be ok with that.

Dianne Dixon: Senior Director, Business Operations PGA TOUR First Tee Foundation, Inc. Originally from Alamogordo, NM she played junior golf and college golf, two years at Northern Arizona University and two years at University of New Mexico. She won the New Mexico State High School Championship in 1995 and New Mexico Women's State Amateur Championship in 2000. Her lowest competitive round is 8-under 64 at the age of 16. Offered a full ride golf scholarship (except for books) to LSU and turned it down because she was too scared to pursue it (they were ranked 6th in the country at the time).

How can parents most effectively support their child(ren) as a junior athlete(s)? What is one piece of advice you have for a junior athlete?

"If you learn to walk 6 feet on your hands, then you can play," my father said as I begged him to sign up for soccer around the age of 9. I came home from school and practiced for about a week and then gave up. "Oh well, I'll pick a different sport...this is too hard" I said to myself. We had one rule in our home around sports, and it was you had to play a sport while in high school. We knew this simple rule early on. After my lack-luster attempt at walking on my hands, I moved on to sampling other sports on my own. I dreamed of taking Jerry Rice's spot on the San Francisco 49ers team and caught my own football passes in the backyard. I pretended to sink a free-throw in the final minutes of a basketball game in front of our house and my tennis serve against the side of our brick home winning the US Open. In those moments, I decided I wanted to be an athlete, but I did not know what kind.

I tried out for the volleyball team in 8th grade and did not make it. Instead, I was made team manager, but the coach let me practice with the team. I started getting better and was soon starting at games. Needless to say, I did not make any friends with my teammates and quickly associated playing volleyball with being bullied. I never told my parents the real reason why I didn't want to try out for the high school volleyball team nor return the high school coach's calls the summer before my freshman year asking me to attend summer camp. Now here I was weeks before starting high school and did not have a sport picked out, so I simply signed up for the golf team to comply with the rule. I sat outside the coach's office on the first day of practice contemplating how I found myself in this situation thinking it couldn't get any worse when three girls from the volleyball team showed up to play, too. My life was over.

Learning you couldn't just run away from your problems and had to face them, was earth shattering. I had no choice at this point. It was the spring and no more sports were available to me. I moved forward and quickly found peace in the solitude of golf. Yes, it was a team sport, but also a place where I could be left alone. I started dreaming of making the final putt to win something (I had no idea what you could win in golf as I had never paid attention to it on tv) and within a year I had improved considerably. Soon after that I noticed I had potential as did others and perhaps my dream of being an athlete would come true.

There are a few key points to call out in this story. The entire time, I was making the decisions. There were a few basic principles my parents had put in place, but I didn't recognize them at the time. The door and opportunity for golf was always open. Next my parents reinforced that if you really cared about something you would be willing to work hard for it. My father would have let me play soccer and supported my efforts to learn to walk on my hands, if my actions demonstrated that's what I wanted to do. This is one of the best lessons my father taught me. Lastly, throughout the process I was learning life lessons even though I didn't always recognize it at the time. The beauty of sports and golf!

Coach Sean Mims: Co-Founder and Director of HoopsEDU, successful basketball coach at every level from recreation league to college and presently coaches the Upward Stars Southeast Adidas 3SSB AAU team. In addition, Coach Mims has 16 years of classroom teaching experience.

How can parents most effectively support their child(ren) as a junior athlete(s)? As a parent, supporting junior athletes is key from an emotional and mental standpoint. Just being there can be the biggest "win" for the athlete.   As the parent, really make sure that you understand the level of love the junior athlete has for the sport(s) he or she is participating in. Some athletes are doing it for fun to be with friends, while others are looking to take it to various levels in competition. Allow the coach(es) to coach the athlete and not you from the stands or sideline. Be sure that all understand the academic requirements of the participating sports and stay on top of schoolwork. It's not all left up to the coaches and teachers. The technology allows that info to be accessed fairly easily.

Last thing of many is to remember that the end goal doesn't happen overnight. Don't put the pressure on the athlete to get a scholarship or a medal because a parent thinks that's motivation. Help the athlete establish a good work ethic, being punctual, and being accountable for his or her work on and off the playing field. That way, it can't be blamed on anyone.

What is one piece of advice you have for a junior athlete? My advice to junior athletes is work on your craft in the sport that you are playing. It's okay to work when no one else is, ask questions when you don't understand, and observe and obtain knowledge to make you mentally, physically, and emotionally better in your craft. Don't compare yourself to anyone but instead create a standard of your own that you are willing to hold yourself accountable to. Never think the classroom is a place of rest. It's just the opposite. It's a place that requires time and effort that will allow you to succeed at your sport. Last, understand that mannerisms matter. Don't let that fall by the wayside.

Coach Larry Campbell: Legendary high school football coach in Lincoln County Georgia for 44 years. "Larry Legend" as he is known to many crafted a superlative career from which he retired in 2013 as the nation's third-winningest high school football coach (according to the NFHS' National High School Sports Record Book) with a 477-85-3 win-loss record. In addition, he led the program to 11 Georgia High School Association (GHSA) state championships in 20 title-game appearances. The NFHS formally recognized Campbell's coaching excellence in 2000 when it inducted him into its National High School Hall of Fame. Played high school football, basketball, baseball and track and went on to play baseball for two years at Anderson Junior

College (SC).

How can parents most effectively support their child(ren) as a junior athlete(s)? First of all, let the coach be the coach. It's hard to be the parent of the child who doesn't always get to play but supports the coach and the athlete. Parents have to make sure their children are playing sports because the child wants to play. Parents can't live their lives through their children. If the child isn't enjoying the sport then don't make them do it. Make sure it's fun for the kids - encourage them to do well and discourage them from quitting. Finally, many parents put pressure on kids at this age that the children don't need - they spend a wad of money on coaches, events, and equipment and should ask themselves if it is really worth it. Parents can ruin a child when they make them do something they don't want to do. Kids are only kids once. Don't make them have unneeded pressure from a parent who wants their child to play a sport that doesn't interest the child. Understand that athletics is not for everyone ... and that is OK. A quote that I think sums this up well is from baseball player and manager Mike Matheny, 'Sports should be about kids and their passion, not about parents and their goals.'

What is one piece of advice you have for a junior athlete? Enjoy and have fun - I don't see kids 'playing' anymore - just playing pickup games of basketball in the yard. Everything is so 'organized' now which I think makes it all so much more formal and robs the kids of the pure joy of the sport and what it can teach. Enjoy being a teenager and don't let your sport take away your fun.

Tami Matheny: Mental Game Coach and founder of Refuse2LoseCoaching, coached collegiate Men's and Women's Tennis, played basketball and tennis collegiately at Lenoir-Rhyne College where she earned a degree in psychology and then a Master's degree in sports administration from University of North Carolina. Author of The Confident Athlete and This is Good!, she can be found at www. r2lc.com.

How can parents most effectively support their child(ren) as a junior athlete(s)?

- Establish effective communication - find out when and how your child wants to hear from you after competition (ask ahead of time not during an emotional moment). Also being able to listen without trying to always solve their problems or agreeing with them (ie. agreeing how bad a coach is or talking about other athletes, parents, etc).
- Be role models for how you want them to act. If you want them to be positive, check your talk. Do you complain about your job or boss - if so what example are you setting? If you want them to eat better, how are you eating, etc.
- Let it be their journey.
- Help them establish their why - what is the bigger picture of what they are doing (again theirs not yours).
- If you have discussions with coaches don't hide it from your athlete - this creates distrust on all fronts.
- The most effective parenting is the triangle - parents, coaches, and athletes take responsibility for their areas and don't get out of their lane and work together, not against each other.

What is one piece of advice you have for a junior athlete?

- Know your why and don't sacrifice it for short term results.
- Remember it's not life or death - learn to keep things in perspective.
- If you are serious about your sport, learn to commit on 3 levels - verbally, physically, and emotionally.
- Practice the mental skills - especially confidence and staying in the moment.

Todd Webber: Owner of ByPass Golf (Spartanburg, SC), Parent of two children who played golf on full scholarship at College of Charleston. Played college golf at Wofford College (Class of 1984)

How can parents most effectively support their child(ren) as a junior athlete(s)? First thing as a parent I had to learn how to be a spectator. I think as a spectator we have to control our emotions and remember it's about the child and not about the parent. Golf is a game - it doesn't really define who we are. It takes patience to play the game of golf but even more to be a spectator! Second, I would not play in every single tournament that comes your way - be more selective and practice and prepare for those events. And I would also choose other things to do during the year boating, fishing, hiking, or riding bikes. As parents we need to let our children be children and not some kind of golf robot.

What is one piece of advice you have for a junior athlete? The best advice I could give is if you decide to play in college choose the college on the school you prefer and what you want to study. And not on golf alone it can save on time and money. Remember only one percent make it to the pro ranks.

Heather Brown: Entering 14th season as Head Coach, Women' Golf, Appalachian State University where she also played collegiately 1984-1988 and was team MVP and Captain in 1988. Native of Connecticut, Brown has 18 years of professional golf experience including leading junior golf programs, mentoring young golfers, and serving as golf professional at various clubs.

How can parents most effectively support their child(ren) as a junior athlete(s)? Parents can encourage their children to enjoy the process of developing in their particular sport. Parents can teach their kids to set up healthy goals and keep them accountable to those goals. Parents can help their child to understand the value of being a coachable player and positive teammate. As the child develops and the sport becomes more competitive a parent must continue to applaud their child for their effort not the result.

What is one piece of advice you have for a junior athlete? You will learn more from your failures than your success. Always stay in the growth mindset.

John Sterling: Owner of Sterling Ventures & Foxfire Software, former VP of Global Sales for Datastream Systems, Inc. Author of Sales for Noobs. John captained the Citadel basketball team in college, played against Michael Jordan and Magic Johnson, and played professionally in Ireland.

How can parents most effectively support their child(ren) as a junior athlete(s)? Take the time at least once a year to go away and discuss the big picture together – even with a 3rd party life planner type if you can. The youngster needs to understand the concept of his/her lifeline, where they are now and what this sports effort will/can make toward ROL (rest of life). Is it your life's work? Doubtful. Does it develop your character for the future, is it fun, do you meet many of your life friends, do you learn good habits, do you get a scholarship, etc? … Sports success can be many great things. Even if you are the greatest, Ali, Jordan, Nicklaus, Tiger - active sports ends. Who are you on purpose becoming and how does this sports work fit into that? I gave too much importance to basketball big time. I played through college and in Europe but by 23 years old, was done – finito. Would have been smarter to see it for what it was versus "going to be the best ever" bravado.

What is one piece of advice you have for a junior athlete? The more tourneys you can play against the better/best competition the better you will be. Fight to play the best even if you are taking some lumps. You will magically improve much faster than just self practice. I got real comfy scoring 40 a game in 1A SC basketball. Need to go to wherever the best are, at least some of the time.

Hernan Chousa: Author of My Son The Tennis Player and ParentShift, Former Tennis Professional (ATP 297), and CEO of Chousa S.R.L.

How can parents most effectively support their child(ren) as a junior athlete(s)? Parents have to be available when they require us and be prepared to give our best to keep being a source of guidance. We need clear boundaries between their space and ours. We need a personal project outside our son or daughter's sport to clear our minds. Always talk positively and be very aware of what we speak because we are their first role model.

What is one piece of advice you have for a junior athlete? I will say to him or her to listen to their inner voice. Many people tell what it's best to do and maybe with good intention. After many years in the sports field, I think or realized that the player has the main answer, and in life too. If he wants to play a sport, he will find the internal drive to succeed no matter what.

Hank Yates: Client manager, Octagon Golf Division, High school All-State honors in baseball and hockey in Arizona, D1 baseball player at University of Delaware, 9th round draft pick of the Los Angeles Dodgers (2013), former minor league baseball player.

How can parents most effectively support their child(ren) as a junior athlete(s)?

- Every relationship is unique between a child and their parent, so there is no cookie cutter formula. I feel for parents with their junior athletes because all they want is what's best for their child and for their child to succeed. Whether I am coaching travel baseball or walking the course with a parent, I see how their child's performance affects them. It's important for parents to understand that this is not their journey, they are there to support their child.

- Lead by example. If the parent is riding an emotional rollercoaster during competition, you can bet the child is, too. Be the person you want your child to be. Respect the coaches, the officials, and other teams. Conduct yourself how you want your child to conduct themselves.

- Parents have to understand that this is their child's journey and it has to come from them, the athlete. The passion, the desire to compete and work hard, has to come from the child. The Serena Williams or Tiger Woods father roles are the worst part about their stories. Parents now believe they have to drag their kid out to practice, 24/7, because that's what it takes. That couldn't be any further from the truth and can cause a lot of tension in your relationship. Those are unique instances and also, most players will not be generational talents. Make sure to enjoy the process with your child, not force it on them.

  - A perfect example is Wayne Gretzky. In an interview he said, almost every parent comes up to me with the same question, how many hours a day did I practice growing up? They ask this because they want to turn to their child and say, see you need to be working 3+ hours a day to be the best. But Wayne never saw practice as work. He just always wanted to play sports. He had a passion for hockey and talent, those two ingredients normally create success.

- Read. Reading books like Mindset by Carol Dweck, or John Wooden's book on leadership, can grow your understanding of the game and coaching. You need to be your child's coach, not just in sports but in life too.

- Stay away from yelling. If you have to yell to get your point across, then you are not communicating effectively. Nobody wants to miss a shot, or strikeout. As long as your child is playing their hardest and focused, that's all they can control. Instead of yelling, teach them. This goes for coaches too!! I have been around a lot of coaches who yell at players. The one thing they all have in common, they are not knowledgeable about their sport. The best coaches will pull the player aside and teach them, because failures are opportunities for growth.

What is one piece of advice you have for a junior athlete?

- Set goals. If you are truly passionate about your sport and want to compete at a high level you need to set goals. Without them, it's like getting in your car and driving with no destination. If you set goals, especially high goals, you will work hard to achieve them. There is no way around it, to get to the top you have to work hard at being the best version of yourself.

Abby Ross: Team USA Futures Program Field Hockey Coach, CEO of Curriki.org

How can parents most effectively support their child(ren) as a junior athlete(s)? Take a genuine interest in their sport. Learn the rules, watch professional matches, ask them questions about strategies and players. This builds a connection of support while distancing an important part of how your junior athlete is constructing their identity and individual connection with the sport. The most impactful relationships I saw from athletes with their parents were when the parents were supportive through curiosity.

What is one piece of advice you have for a junior athlete? Being a model teammate can bring you to a next level of purpose and fulfillment in a sport. Things like celebrating the success of others, encouraging and pointing out strengths of others, thanking your coaches and officials. It is often an overlooked component of competing and winning, but knowing that you are celebrated for your inner character and ways you've lifted up others unlocks the next level of motivation and performance.

Bethany Poppe: Head boy's and girl's tennis coach at Byrnes High School (SC) for 5 and 7 years, respectively. Coached boys' and girls' middle and JV high school tennis at the Pingry School in Martinsville, N.J., and was the head middle school coach (girls and boys) in the Oak Hills School District in Cincinnati, OH. Played four years of DII intercollegiate tennis at Newberry College (SC) and still plays and captains several USTA women's and mixed teams.

How can parents most effectively support their child(ren) as a junior athlete(s)? With sports like golf, tennis and many other individual sports, parents can support their children as junior athletes by building independence in a few ways. First, a large part of confidence on the court, course or field comes from preparation. Because parents are most often on the sideline and play a non-communicative role during their actual game or practice (due to rules, coaching expectations, etc.), players are left to work through adversity on their own. Athletes, especially junior athletes, often can't run to the sideline during a sporting event to ask their parents for something else to drink, to wear their hat or sunglasses or ask if their parents brought an item they use or need for their event.

Therefore, preparation starts at home. As a coach, I often see that parents pack their child's athletic bag with equipment they need, their clothing or uniform and even their snacks and drinks. However, when a parent forgets something or the child can't find something in their bag, they turn to their parent with anger and frustration for not providing them with what they need to perform. Oftentimes, the parent then assumes responsibility for the missing item and the athlete blames their parent for a lack of preparation, which inevitably leaves behind a lack of confidence that affects the player, parent, coach and often the team.

While it is important for an athlete to have what they need to perform, parents should foster independence by teaching and expecting their child to prepare and pack their own gear as both a part of preparation (which translates into confidence in their athletic event) and to help preserve the child-parent relationship.

To provide additional independence and grow confidence, parents should consider running through scenarios wherein their child will face adversity in their athletic event. What will you do if you break the strings on your racket during a point? How will you traverse a water obstacle that you have already shot two balls into? What will you do if your shoelace breaks during a competition? Parents can't work through these challenges while their athlete is playing, but this type of problem solving and preparation allows the athlete to become more comfortable facing adversity as an individual.

What is one piece of advice you have for a junior athlete? This may seem like a "duh" response since they likely play that sport and have an understanding of the mechanics and scoring or game knowledge needed to succeed. However, performance as we see it on the course or field is only a small fraction of the work that is needed to perform. I have found that many athletes train in one way... by actually playing the sport. While this is crucial to build muscle memory and confidence, we have to consider the mental, tactical, and technical needs of our sport, which can require endurance or aerobic training (both physical and mental as both can be exhausting during an athletic event).

In addition, stretching, diet, hydration and sleep are all items to know and consider as you work to elevate your game play. Having a well-rounded understanding of your sport and working to train all aspects is where we see tremendous growth. Yet, many athletes feel that preparation and training shut off when we walk off-court or field and it resumes only when we return.

Don Yaeger: Award-winning keynote speaker, business leadership coach, author of nearly 30 books including eleven New York Times best-sellers and a recent USA Today best-seller ***Best Seat in the House*** with Jack Nicklaus II, and his most recent ***Up and Down: Victories and Struggles in the Course of Life*** with Bubba Watson, and longtime Associate Editor for Sports Illustrated. Don is primarily sought to discuss lessons on achieving greatness, learned from first-hand experiences with some of the greatest sports legends in the world. Learn more about Don and his great collection of resources and books at *www.donyaeger.com*.

How can parents most effectively support their child(ren) as a junior athlete(s)? The athletes I know who most enjoyed their careers at every level had similar experiences with youth sports – parents and coaches who focused on how they participated rather than the outcome of the contest. If they gave their best and the outcome was a loss, the effort not the outcome was the discussion on the drive home. Several told me their parents made sure to ask "did you have fun?" This is not to be mistaken for a "participation award" mentality. It was simply an intentional effort to encourage their child's want to through measured reaction.

What is one piece of advice you have for a junior athlete? Be a great teammate. If others enjoy you being there, you'll find a spot on every team.

Michael J. Ross, Ph.D., ABPP: Professor of Psychology, Director, Saint Louis University Sport Psychological Sciences and Consultation Lab www.slu.edu/arts-and-sciences/psychology/center-clinics/sports-psych.php

How can parents most effectively support their child(ren) as a junior athlete(s)? Young athletes are motivated by encouragement more than criticism. Criticism leads to fear of failure while encouragement leads to motivation to achieve success. I prefer the "sandwich" approach when coaching or correcting young athletes. The sandwich approach means beginning with praise--what the athlete did well (e.g., "you bent your knees well and kept your eye on the ball"). Then give correction with specific coaching suggestions (e.g., "next time, follow through all the way with your swing"). Finish with encouragement (e.g., "you can do this").

What is one piece of advice you have for a junior athlete? Focus on your performance rather than just the outcome (i.e., winning). Being an athlete is an important part of your identity, but it is only one part of you. Your identity as an athlete is grounded and framed by values that you hold and can articulate. Intrinsic or internal motivation leads to better performance and helps to sustain effort particularly during times of adversity. External rewards or pressures can reduce intrinsic motivation; consequently, know your "why" as an athlete. Most successful athletes are internally motivated by their love and passion for their sport rather than others' expectations.

Angie Ridgeway, LPGA, TPI: In 17th year as Head Coach, Women's Golf, for Wofford College. Played college golf at Appalachian State and 16 years professionally - 4 years on mini tour and 12 years on the LPGA.

How can parents most effectively support their child(ren) as a junior athlete(s)? By providing the opportunity to play and consistent, positive reinforcement. Don't push, let the athlete figure out their level of love for their sport. I've seen plenty of junior golf parents get this wrong.

Maintaining a stable presence of positivity is of equal importance for parents. This is crucial in the development of a junior athlete. A parent's positive body language and relaxed facial expression are priceless when it comes to a junior athlete's confidence and their level of happiness in sport. A happy athlete is usually a more successful athlete!

What is one piece of advice you have for a junior athlete? If at all possible, I think junior athletes should play more than one sport through 9th grade. It's good for physical development and good for character development. Learning to handle the highs and lows in more than one sport should make for a more emotionally stable junior athlete.

Also, I like the idea of a young athlete teaching their sport to a younger junior, whether it's casually one-on-one, or by helping with a camp or clinic. This helps the young athlete realize how much they've accomplished to that point and grows their confidence by helping another kid learn a new sport.

Garrison Hearst: Record setting running back at University of Georgia from 1990-1992. Hearst was a consensus All-America selection, the Doak Walker Award recipient, ESPN's ESPY Winner for Outstanding Collegiate Athlete and SEC Player of the year in 1992. He finished third in the Heisman Trophy voting. First-round draft pick by the Arizona Cardinals, he played 10 seasons in the NFL, running for 1,000 yards in four different seasons and was named NFL Comeback Player of the Year in 2001.

How can parents most effectively support their child(ren) as a junior athlete(s)? There are many things they can do as parents - one is to support the process and not just the game. Whatever the sport, make sure the kid is putting in the work needed to be great. Give him or her as much support through whatever access you can provide. (weights, track, trainers, nutrition, etc.) Allow for tough coaching because the next level will be even harder - and life is full of tough times! Be supportive but allow them to fight through the ups and downs of sport without trying to be a fixer!

What is one piece of advice you have for a junior athlete? No one should have to make you train, eat right or do the off the field things needed to be great! With so many resources through social media you can get tricks and lessons that we did not have! Take advantage of all the things in your world to be great!

Thomas Ray Williams: 2008 graduate of the University of Southern California with a degree in Sociology where, as a linebacker, he captained a Trojan team that amassed a record of 59-6, 2 National Championships and 3 Rose Bowls - and in addition earning him the nickname "The Hitman". Thomas was drafted 155th overall in 2008 and went on to play 5 years in the NFL where he was not just focused on winning and competing, but rather mastering TEAMWORK, MENTAL TOUGHNESS and LEADERSHIP. In 2012 after a career ending neck injury, Thomas transitioned from a game changer to a life changer, helping people tackle obstacles and finding their winning solutions. Williams is now a motivational speaker and Director of his nonprofit Pursuits of Greatness. He has traveled worldwide speaking to different corporations, athletes and students on how to "fully maximize their potential." In 2014 Thomas published his autobiography, Permission to DREAM and has since published The Relentless Pursuit of Greatness. Both great resources are available on Amazon and at www.thomasrwilliams.com.

How can parents most effectively support their child(ren) as a junior athlete(s)? Pay attention to what lights your junior athlete up ... when they go to practice and games and the way the coach is coaching them - do they respond well and react to affirmation, correction and/ or discipline? If you can notice those nuances of your child in the sports when they 'get to play'... then you will be able to parent your child in that same way most appropriately and effectively ... I think one of the most important things a coach can do is to understand the 'person' and then coach that 'person' through sports.

Same thing on the flip side of that, you get an opportunity to have a conversation with your child outside of homework, chores - outside of the cliches ... 'how was practice?' and if you go to a practice or game ... you aren't just paying attention to your child when they are on the tee box or the pitcher's mound or during the play on a football field - you are actually paying attention to them between the 14th and 15th holes, what is their reaction like, how are they responding? What is their body language like when they are down and out? When they just triple bogeyed a hole or as a pitcher they just walked three consecutive batters ... how do they react when they face disappointments? When you can pay attention to not just the parts of the game that are obvious ... but you can also pay attention to the little nuances as well - it is powerful.

What is one piece of advice you have for a junior athlete? I received great advice at every different level. The life changing advice I wish I had gotten a little earlier was having someone speak to me about the 'life after sports' a little bit more. The more I was able to talk about it, the more I thought about it, and the more I was able to understand the nuances of life after sports while I was playing my sport - I think the more it makes for more of a rounded human being.

Bud Cronin: Former Head Golf Coach and Assistant Basketball Coach at University of Oklahoma, played basketball collegiately at University of South Carolina. Self-described giver of 'old school' advice, Bud gave us both questions in a single narrative below.

How can parents most effectively support their child(ren) as a junior athlete(s)? You asked for my comments on how parents should handle their young athletes. Being 80 years old I am from the old school so what I say may not apply in today's world.

My parents never saw me play a game of basketball until the State of West Virginia finals at WVU in 1958 nor attended any practices from seventh grade and beyond. I earned a full scholarship at University of South Carolina and started my freshman, junior, and senior year and they never saw me play a single game. It never bothered me and I gave it no thought as I was playing the game for my enjoyment, not theirs.

I caddied in the Ohio Open and saw first-hand Jack Nicklaus beat all the pros and amateurs in Ohio as a 16-year-old. His dad, Charlie, brought him there but stayed in the background out of sight but still kind of kept up with things. He was not near or on the field of play where Jack could see his emotions and expressions. That impressed me then and I have tried to be there for my kids but wanted to be sure that they did not feel they were performing for me, and they enjoyed their experience. Only thing I ever asked them was 'did they have fun?'

Jen Brooks, CMMA: Founder/CEO, The Global Community of Women in High School Sports www.globalcommunityofwomeninsports.com

How can parents most effectively support their child(ren) as a junior athlete(s)? A parent can most effectively support their child athlete by walking the sports journey with them but from behind rather than leading their child. Let the athlete charter their own path and at their own pace. Provide support when requested. Keep personal desires and wishes from your own personal experience out of the journey. Constantly ask your child if they are enjoying it - are they having fun? The minute the answer is no, or they are slow to answer yes, it is time to reevaluate the journey you are on. Remember this is not about you or your happiness but rather that of your child's.

What is one piece of advice you have for a junior athlete? Have fun! If you are not having fun, ask yourself, why are you doing what you are doing? Also, it is okay even necessary to take time off and allow your body to rest. It is not a sign of weakness to rest but rather shows maturity on your part.

Leslie Trujillo, M.A.: Kinesiology/Health Professor at Los Angeles Harbor College. She is also an Athletic Performance and Mindset Coach. Leslie has trained Heisman Trophy winners, All-Americans, and National Championship teams at LMU, Notre Dame, University of Southern California, and at The Yard Performance Center. She has her B.S. in Exercise Science from UNM, M.A. in Education from LMU, M.A. in Kinesiology: Sports Management from CSULB, and her Certificate in Sport Psychology from SDUIS. She played Division I tennis at UNM. Leslie is a Master Trainer with ZHealth Performance, specializing in movement and the nervous system. She has worked with thousands of youth, high school, collegiate, and professional athletes who are committed to their life and performance goals. She conducts team training, motivational talks & programs, team-building events, seminars, camps & clinics. Leslie is the director of the CHAMPS (Challenging Athlete's Minds For Personal Success) program at LHAC to help student-athletes succeed in academics and athletics.

To learn more about Leslie "Coach C's" performance training, go to www.lesliectrujillo.com. In addition, she hosts the Podcast The Developing Athlete and co-authored the book, DEAR HER: Letters to teenage girls and young ladies on lessons learned through education, athletics, and life available on Amazon.

How can parents most effectively support their child(ren) as a junior athlete(s)? The most important thing for a parent to do for a junior athlete is to allow them to understand that you will love them no matter what - no matter if they are the highest scorer, lowest scorer, or don't even see a lot of playing time. Parents need to support the journey of the student-athlete, appreciating that the person comes first. Remember that it is a journey, a journey of development and they don't have to be absolutely perfect or great today. Introduce them to the tools and environment that will help them grow and succeed and then allow them to grow throughout those experiences. Their experience is not necessarily the parent's experience. One of my favorite sayings is that your struggle will become your strength. Know that your child(ren) is(are) going to have struggles. We as parents can not just take away the struggle, all we can do is support them as they grow through it. If they can grow through it on their own, they will grow stronger. If we save them all the time, they might not gain the strength they need to fly as high as they can.

What is one piece of advice you have for a junior athlete? Take full responsibility for your development as a person, as a student, and as an athlete. Your success is not dependent on your parents, coaches, teammates, or anyone else. They can provide the tools and the way, but it is up to you to take full advantage and capitalize on all the opportunities. Are you maximizing your skill work, strength and conditioning, sleep/recovery, nutrition, and mindset? Look at your daily habits and see if they match your vision for yourself. If your habits do not match your goals, you only have two choices: You can choose to upgrade your habits to get you closer to your goals or you are going to have to choose to lower your goals. You can make any choice you want, just know that every choice has some consequence (positive or negative)...and you can always choose again... and you can choose to ask for help. Whatever you are going through, you are never alone. Someone has gone through what you are going through and can help you travel forward and find your strength. Enjoy the journey.

Brandon Barden: Standout tight-end at Vanderbilt University and spent several years in the NFL with the Tennessee Titans, Jacksonville Jaguars, Kansas City Chiefs, and Dallas Cowboys.

How can parents most effectively support their child(ren) as a junior athlete(s)? In my opinion a parent's role in a child's development from an athletic standpoint is very crucial. If a parent is too demanding a child might become discouraged and the "fun" might diminish. On the other hand, if a parent doesn't push their child then going through the motions will seem like a normal activity for the child and the drive to get better might fall away. I come from a very competitive family. My mom was a coach and one of the most competitive people I've ever been around. Automatically that mentality was transferred down to me. My mom was the parent in the stands yelling when I struck out at baseball, missed a free throw in basketball, or when I threw an interception in football. Yes, we had our arguments from the field to the stands before but looking back I wouldn't change it for anything. She is the reason I got to the level I did. She encouraged me but also gave me strict criticism when I needed it most. Without the constructive criticism, areas of needed improvement, along with the support to fix them, I wouldn't have ever been asked to write this piece now.

Everyone learns differently, everyone has different athletic abilities, but at the end of the day if the child doesn't have the intrinsic motivation to improve then pure athleticism will only take you so far. I didn't want to be mediocre. I didn't want to get a trophy for participation. I wanted to win at everything I did and a lot of that attitude was passed down from my parents. I am very grateful for their support throughout the years.

What is one piece of advice you have for a junior athlete? The best piece of advice I could give a young athlete is to work on the fundamentals at the sport of choice. Everyone wants to hit a homerun, drive a golf ball 300 yards, or shoot 3 pointers like a pro but not everyone focuses on the "little things" that have the greatest impact for success. Most sports have a very artistic feature to them. For instance, once you understand a golf swing and what affects the ball flight you know the fundamentals of just the swing and can adjust things as needed. The same goes for a baseball swing. Every sport has key fundamentals that need great focus before you can become an elite player.

Sam Brooks: Supervisor of Personalized Learning Putnam County Schools (TN), ESPN Football Analyst (OVC), played High School basketball and football then Division 1 football on scholarship at Tennessee Tech University as a four-year starter. High school coach for 16 years and father of an accomplished golfer (Will) who played collegiately and is now pursuing a professional career.

How can parents most effectively support their child(ren) as a junior athlete(s)? I have been a high school coach for 16 years in the state of Tennessee and a parent of a very successful HS and college athlete. I have a unique perspective on the role of a parent with a junior athlete. I believe parents should simply be the support system for their child in whatever sport they choose. I played college football and I think that created some pressure on my son to do the same. Once he found out that I would support him in what he chose to play, he excelled at his chosen sport and I supported him in every way possible to help him achieve the goals he had set forth for himself. I have seen my share of parents who live through their child's career and can't separate the action of the game from the fact they are the parent and should always provide a level head and comfort to their aspiring athlete.

What is one piece of advice you have for a junior athlete? It has to be FUN! If you do not enjoy it or you are doing it for someone else, find something that YOU like. Life is too short to put this much time into something you do not enjoy. Realizing sports will teach you how to deal with good times and bad times is a key to keeping the right attitude and learning from your successes and especially your mistakes. My son has had an incredible time in golf since he was seven years old and he has ALWAYS loved the game. He will take the next leap this August by turning Pro and trying to make his way to one of the professional tours. The greatest thing about it is he loves the game as much today as he did when he was seven years old. It is important to LOVE what you do and work as hard as possible to achieve your goals.

Eric Reyes: Former high school football coach, creator and host of the Hey Coach! Podcast where business concepts are discussed leveraging viewpoints from the athletic sidelines, and former partner at William J O'Reilly Inc Brokerage firm.   www.listennotes.com/podcasts/hey-coach-eric-reyes-TiSfoJrvRMQ/

How can parents most effectively support their child(ren) as a junior athlete(s)? Make sure the athlete is well rounded. Having them not only play other sports to allow for strength and recovery of their body but to have outside interests and outside friends. My son played college football and he decided to join a fraternity. When I asked him why he did it when he has all his player friends he told me he wanted friends that had nothing to do with football. He wanted to talk and hang out with other people doing other things. It was a release from the day-to-day grind. The second is listening to the athlete. Parents sometimes get caught up in helping the athlete so much that they push and push to the point the athlete is playing for the parent and not for them. I have friends that had their boys playing year-round baseball and in college they quit the team. It wasn't fun anymore. If they need a break, they need a break.

What is one piece of advice you have for a junior athlete? The piece of advice for the athlete goes a bit with the first part. Find out what else you truly enjoy. It never is just the sport. Even professional athletes search for other things they are passionate about. Why wait to find that passion - try new things. And remember - Have Fun. You only live once.

Jeff Heggie - Success Coach: Jeff is a former professional rodeo cowboy and has over twenty years of experience coaching basketball. Today,

Jeff is an entrepreneur and Success Coach with a passion for helping others achieve their biggest dreams. Jeff starts with a focus on mindset to help clients and businesses get to the next level and break through the mental and physical barriers that hold them back. Jeff and his wife, Tamara, both grew up in Southern Alberta but now make Arizona home. Family and sports have always been important to him, and he loves spending time coaching or watching his kids. linkedin.com/in/jeffheggie, Facebook/Instagram: JeffHeggieCoaching, www.jeffheggie.com/ConfidentAthlete, jeffheggie.com, beacons.ai/jeffheggiecoaching, email jeff@jeffheggie.com.

How can parents most effectively support their child(ren) as a junior athlete(s)? Junior athletes all have their different goals and dreams. But whether they talk about it or not, they all have one similar goal. They want their parent(s) to support them and to be proud of them! It wasn't until I was a coach and a parent of young athletes that I realized just how much support I had as an athlete growing up. With two brothers who were also multi-sport athletes, somehow, I always had a parent there to support me. Whether it was rushing me out of the ring after a boxing match to get me to my hockey game, driving me 16 hours to compete at the Silver State International Rodeo, or just being in the stands at every basketball game I knew I could depend on them.

As a coach I notice the parents who are there supporting their children. I also notice those who aren't. I know that life gets busy and sometimes work schedules make it impossible. But it's the parents that could be there but are not that break my heart.

Kids crave their parent's approval and support. They need it. When they are playing a sport they love but get nothing from their parents, it hurts. There are so many ways that a parent can effectively support their child(ren) as a junior athlete(s). This is important for a child because it has such an impact on the rest of their life. Many life lessons and habits are developed through their experiences as an athlete.

Parents have a major impact on whether their child develops a fixed mindset or a growth mindset. They are influenced by how the parent acts in the stands and talks to the coaches. How a parent talks to and treats their child when they are successful and when they fail teaches a lot. This isn't a simple question with a simple answer. There are many different things that we could discuss, and they are all important. But I feel that the most effective way that a parent can support their child(ren) as a junior athlete(s) is to show them that they care. It doesn't mean you have to coach their team. It doesn't mean that you have to be at every single game. But if they know that you are interested and they are important to you, it will mean so much to them.

What is one piece of advice you have for a junior athlete? There are two questions I ask all my athletes to answer:

- Why do you play?
- Who are you playing for?

As young athletes develop their skills and talent, things begin to change. How good could they be? Will they play Division One? Is there a professional career in their future?

It's important for junior athletes to remember WHY they play.

One summer my daughter was playing for two different club basketball teams plus our provincial team, Team Alberta. It was a lot! I feared that it might be too much, and she could get burned out. I remember picking her up after a practice - it was the second two-hour practice of the night, and she was exhausted. She flopped down in the passenger seat of my truck and let out a big sigh. Then she said, "sometimes I forget how much I love this game!" She was playing because she loved it.

Knowing who you are playing for is an important question to ask. I've watched athletes with a lot of talent and potential get pushed so hard by a coach or a parent that they lose their love for the sport. It's not fun anymore. But they feel like they have to keep giving 110% because they don't want to disappoint their parent(s) or coach.

I'm a big believer in hard work and dedication. If you want to be your best, you have to put in the work. But for a junior athlete to reach their full potential they need to have a strong "why," and they have to begin playing for themselves.

Asia Mape: Founder of Ilovetowatchyouplay.com and 4-time Emmy Award-winning journalist and Sports Television Producer and former D1 basketball player. She's covered the most high-profile sporting events in the world, including five Olympics, multiple NBA playoffs, and 2 Super Bowls. She's interviewed hundreds of athletes and has helped tell their stories of incredible talent, work ethic, and their journeys to become world-class competitors. The mother of three daughters who play sports, Asia has dedicated the greater part of the last 12-years to her daughters' various activities, a combination of club soccer, basketball, field hockey, volleyball, and water polo. She has schlepped her kids to some 7-8 practices a week, attended tournaments or games most weekends. Most of the time, she has loved it, but along the way, she often wondered whether there wasn't a better way. This question was the genesis of ILoveToWatchYouPlay.com. She hopes you will find in this website; humor, compassion, and guidance for raising healthy, happy, and successful young athletes while maintaining some sort of sanity for your family! You can also sign up for the ILTWYP Newsletter to get all the news, information, and inspiration about youth sports delivered right to your inbox.

How can parents most effectively support their child(ren) as a junior athlete(s)? Crossing the line from supporting to pressuring our kids can be very fine, but when you do it, it's just as impactful as the most aggressive over-the-top parent out there. Once you cross over, it's incredibly hard to come back and repair the damage, but you must try. Because if your child deems that your interest and influence go beyond their happiness and well-being, well - you've already lost them. It may not show itself at 7, 10, 16, or even 20, but eventually, it will. And it's not just quitting or a strained relationship between the child and parent that can occur, it can be subtle, like a slow and steady loss of joy and ownership, that will eventually lead to quitting or resentment.

The most important way parents can support their athlete is to do just that, support. Support looks like love, hugs, excitement, a happy face in the crowd, and a welcoming car ride home - regardless of the outcome on the field. It doesn't look like expecting a return on investment for the time and money spent, it doesn't place sports above family and school and it definitely doesn't look like a steady dose of anger and disappointment. You must trust their process...THEIR process, not your agenda or dreams. Be there to catch them when they fall and congratulate them when they succeed.

What is one piece of advice you have for a junior athlete? Find your joy and hold onto it tightly. It's your journey, not your parents and not your coaches. They may mean well, but protect what you love and what you don't. Do this by finding your voice and letting those around you know how you feel and speaking your truth. Don't hold back trying to keep from hurting feelings or disappointing those around you, this is a losing battle as it will catch up to you and them. If you consistently talk to your parents about your feelings, then it's their responsibility to work within those confines and support you and if they don't, then shame on them. And my most practical advice for athletes - sleep 8-10 hours per night! It affects every aspect of your life and your sports in astounding ways.

Chip Baker - Live. Learn. Serve. Inspire. Go get it!: Teacher and coach for 21 years (4th generation educator), author, speaker, and podcaster. Jon Gordon Power of Positive Leadership trainer, Creator of Chip Baker - Character Development Program, host of The Success Chronicles (a YouTube channel/podcast that interviews people from all walks of life about success), multiple time best-selling author Growing Through Your Go Through, and Effective Conversation To Ignite Relationships among others. youtube.com/c/ChipBakerTheSuccessChronicles, chip-baker-the-success-chronicles.square.site/, Twitter @chipbaker19, and Facebook/Instagram @chipbakertsc

How can parents most effectively support their child(ren) as a junior athlete(s)? Parents can be aware of the information that will allow their child to perform efficiently and effectively. I feel that it is important for the parent to be a parent and support their child by providing positive encouragement and expecting them to give their best efforts all the time. It is important to teach them to be committed and do their part for the team.

What is one piece of advice you have for a junior athlete? You will learn more from your failures than your success. Always stay in the growth mindset. Show up and do the hard stuff every day - it teaches you transferable skills that you will be able to use for the rest of your life.

Coach Paula Kirkland: A critical component of Dorman High School (SC) athletics for 40 years, Coach Kirkland serves as Assistant Athletic Director and Head Volleyball coach. Kirkland also coached Varsity and JV basketball in prior years.

How can parents most effectively support their child(ren) as a junior athlete(s)? I imagine each family system is different so therefore there may not be a cut-and-dried answer. My belief though is to provide unwavering support in their child's effort. I heard a terrible story one time of a parent putting her child on restriction based on her performance in a softball tournament. Much to no one's surprise that athlete quit the sport after she had invested many years in the program. I say that to say this - I believe parents should recognize and acknowledge achievement, it is part of athletics, but to harp on the failures is not inspiring in my opinion. Being there for their kids is important. How can they do that? Here are some thoughts:

- Get them to practice and pick them up on time. When they start driving on their own re-enforce this, it teaches responsibility.
- Leave them, do not watch practice. Allow them their growth opportunities without parental oversight.

- At home, encourage conversation about their practices without comparisons to other players. Encourage conversations about their interactions with their coaches.
- At home parents should refrain from disparaging remarks about their child's teammates and coaches; this does nothing but fosters a negative undercurrent of emotions towards their teammates and coaches. As a coach, I always address this issue with my parent groups at our parent meetings and in email correspondence.
- After games/matches parents should emphasize the positives. Performance errors can be acknowledged but with the intent of exploring, through conversation, what the athlete feels they could've done differently, not what the parent feels the athlete could've done differently. Learning happens often through how you react to mistakes or failures.
- Encourage positive approaches to their mental game and how they interact with their teammates and coaches. This may also include a frank discussion about body language.
- Parents should also encourage their athlete(s) to talk to their coaches. I tell my parents to let their child start being the young adult that I view them as.

What is one piece of advice you have for a junior athlete? The best piece of advice I can give any athlete is to engage their coaches and teammates in as positive a manner as possible. Foster that relationship so that in the best of times and the worst of times you have folks around you that you care about and that care about you too and you can serve each other. Talk to your teammates and coaches, initiate conversations!

Renee Lopez: College Coach for 14 years (NCAA D1, D2, & NAIA Head Coach), former NCAA Compliance Director, and now Recruiting Educator and Author of *Looking For A FULL RIDE?: An Insider's Recruiting Guide. www.lookingforafullride.com* and *www. rlopezcoaching.com*

How can parents most effectively support their child(ren) as a junior athlete(s)? It is important for parents to help kids to enjoy the game, develop sportsmanship, and teach them how to be a good teammate. It is important for a parent to be a parent and not have a post-game analysis criticism of the game during the car ride home. Tell them 'I enjoyed watching you play today.' Ask 'Did you have fun?' & 'How do you feel about grabbing some pizza?'. So many kids burn out from the sport because it is no longer fun and the pressure from adults. We need to teach them how to be coachable and have fun.

What is one piece of advice you have for a junior athlete? Every day, have the mentality that "I am going to get 1% better". It may be an individual technical skill, learning a new tactical approach, getting faster, learning how to make healthy food choices, or how to be a better teammate. These are essential components of any elite athlete.

Keith D. Kostrzewski: Business Strategist and Sports Enthusiast, Executive Consultant, OnCore Golf. Four-sport athlete in high school (soccer, football, hockey and baseball). Played four years of Division I soccer at Providence College, member of the Big East Conference and 3-time Big East All-Academic Team.

How can parents most effectively support their child(ren) as a junior athlete(s)? I don't have first-hand experience (yet) being a parent of a junior athlete, but what I will share are experiences that have impacted my approach going forward.

- This is your child's path, not yours. There is a delicate balance between encouragement/motivation.
- Don't ever hold your sacrifices, expenses, or trade-offs over your child's head. You can instill values that your child appreciates and respects the level of commitment, but it can't be used against them or perceived to be damaging or negative to the family. At the end of the day, as a parent you have made these choices to support your child, and using it against the child can be extremely damaging both to the near term joy for the game, as well as long-term trust and respect.
- Stay in tune to your child's emotions and dig deep when warning signs emerge. Again, it's a delicate balance to instill grit and work ethic, with truly understanding if there's something physically or mentally blocking or restricting development. Children are resilient, but so many have a fear of disappointing their parents or coaches, that they continue on a path that is not enjoyable, and that can not only impact performance, but have negative long-term implications as they develop into young adults
- Ensure that they pay proper attention to academics, social norms, and maintain a healthy dose of reality. The data is clear about the % that achieve greatness (professional, high amateur, collegiate performance) is low. By continuing to ground your child, it has two distinct benefits. One, it helps prepare them for life after the games have ended; and two, it helps them become better leaders on their teams and the type of player that a coach wants to keep around on cut down day. This intangible cannot

be underestimated as competition and importance of culture intensity.

What is one piece of advice you have for a junior athlete?

1. Thank your parents (and siblings)

   As a junior athlete, it's OK to not understand or appreciate the commitment it takes from your support system for you to be successful. But know that it's significant. There is tremendous joy and pride, but it comes with significant trade-offs; personally, professionally, and emotionally that come with this journey. It's part of the job of being a parent, and we love it, but something that will help both sides communicate better and appreciate one another if acknowledged.

2. Don't take this time for granted

   There will never, ever (ever did I say ever) be a time like now for you to dive into your passion, enjoy health, and be void of so many distractions that will allow you to excel in your sport. As much as you can, respect and appreciate that the time is now to focus on athletic and physical excellence, not for the other distractions that can take you down the wrong path.

3. Develop great eating, sleeping, and mindfulness habits

   As a junior athlete, you feel invincible, because you are ... But as you grow, what you eat, how you sleep, and how you take care of your mind, will prove to be just as essential as what you do in the weight room or on the practice field. Trust us on this one. Some addictive behaviors during this time can compound into irreversible patterns. Treat your mind and body like a gift, and it will reward you.

4. Do the hard stuff.

It's hard to run 4 miles after practice. It's hard to go to the weight room on a Saturday morning on an off day. It's hard to say no to the hamburger at 8 o'clock with your friends. It's hard to listen to your coach when you know you are right … But it's pretty true, if you think you should be doing it (or not doing it) - it's probably the right decision.

My regret in my early playing days was not being focused on the cardio and strength work necessary to help me become better at the skill part of my game. Focusing on skill training is critical, but if you have to consider (consciously or subconsciously) your endurance or strength when executing on skill - in most cases you will have lost any advantage gained in skill.

5. Take time to recharge if you fall out of love

If you find yourself losing passion, or more specifically love of the game you're playing, take a step back and recharge. As you progress in your career, the amount of pressure, time commitment, and physical and emotional strain will take its toll. You only survive these challenges if you love what you are doing. If you have that drive to be successful, and truly want to be successful, but feel something is slipping, step back and take some time, and re-center. Don't push until you're at a breaking point.

Remember, there will always be someone better than you. Accept it … but that does not mean that you still can't be great. Comparisons to others never get you anywhere. Use it as motivation, but never as a deterrent.

Coach Dan Horwitz: Leadership Development, Culture & Team Building Consultant, College Recruiting Advisor, and Basketball Coach/Trainer. Dan was a four-year NCAA student athlete and captain at Newbury College and three-year collegiate coach. Author of Help Them Up (available on Amazon) the mission of which is to help educate, energize, and empower players and coaches to build and sustain a championship basketball culture. www.danhorwitz.com/

How can parents most effectively support their child(ren) as a junior athlete(s)? My parents knew very little about the game of basketball when I first started playing when I was five. However, they knew a lot about loving me unconditionally. My parents learned quickly that I had a passion for basketball. They signed me up for teams and camps so I could improve my skills. The first question they would ask after every practice and game was, "Did you have fun?" They knew how competitive sports can be, especially while playing AAU and high school basketball, but they always put the emphasis on having fun. My mom and dad were at almost every single one of my games. Before most games, I would jog over from lay-up lines and give them each a hug and engage in our personalized handshake. They did not care if I started the game or sat on the bench. They just wanted me to know they were there to support me and cheer on the team. They didn't coach me from the sidelines or talk to me at halftime on how I was playing.

The most coaching I would get from afar was an encouraging smile, an affirming head nod, or a thumbs up. After the game, they would ask if I had fun and allow me to talk about whatever I wanted. Even when I was hard on myself or prompted them to ask what I could work on, they focused on what I did well. They praised my effort because they knew I always tried my best which was a mentality they instilled in me at a very young age. A lot of parents would ask my mom, who has four kids, "how do you choose if you should go to a game or go to another obligation?" My mom's consistent reply was always, "The choice is easy because there is no choice. You go to the game. Your kids grow up so fast and before you know it, all of those games will be over." Showing up for your kids, making them feel seen and valued, is the most effective way to support your child. Sports can serve as an amazing platform where a parent and child can create a strong bond that will last a lifetime.

What is one piece of advice you have for a junior athlete? As a junior athlete, I loved to play a lot of sports! I played baseball, basketball, soccer, and football growing up. I don't remember most of the records of those teams I played on but I definitely remember the fun moments I shared with my teammates! If I could give one piece of advice to a junior athlete, I would say it's extremely important to have a "team-first mentality". The "team-first mentality" is when each individual team member finds ways to contribute and benefit the group through their words and actions. They don't let their performance dictate the type of teammate they are on a given day. They are consistent with giving teammates high-fives, encouraging them with their words, and giving their best effort every play. They help teammates up off the ground if they fall over, they offer to show up early or stay late to help a teammate improve a skill, and they celebrate their team's success when on the bench.

Great teammates ask engaging questions and learn about the person on their team, not just the athlete. These are things that great teammates execute consistently because they know they are fully in control of their effort and attitude. These skills translate outside sports and are all qualities that are needed now more than ever in today's society. Make the choice to be a consistently great teammate and continue trying your best! I will be cheering for you!

Coach Jeanne Sutherland: Long-time collegiate head coach, she was named as the Associate Head Coach for the Nebraska Husker women's golf program on July 1, 2021. Sutherland joined Nebraska after spending the past 10 seasons (2011-2021) as the head coach at SMU and prior to that, 15 seasons as the head coach at Texas A&M (1992-2007). Coach Sutherland shares insights, guidance, and practical advice through her blog at https://12monthsofgolfinvail.blogspot.com/.

In 2018, Sutherland was named the inaugural winner of the Women's Golf Coaches Association (WGCA) Kim Evans Award, which is presented annually to the college or high school coach, and Class A PGA Professional, whose support of the game through teaching, coaching and involvement in the community has helped ensure the continued growth of golf, and who represents the finest qualities the sport has to offer. Sutherland also earned the WGCA Founders Award in 2017.

Following her time with the Aggies, Sutherland stepped away from college golf for four years (2007-11) to serve as the Head Professional at the Vail Golf Club in Colorado. She had previously served as an Assistant Golf Professional at Vail for seven years (1985-92).

She earned her bachelor's degree in secondary education (English) from Northern Iowa in 1983, before earning her master's degree in athletic administration from Iowa in 1989. A member of the

University of Northern Iowa Athletic Hall of Fame, Sutherland was named to the 1981 AIAW Division II All-America Team and the 1981 and 1982 AIAW All-Region 6 teams. As a sophomore at the 1981 AIAW Division II National Championships, she grabbed a third-place individual finish and led the Panthers to a third-place team finish. As a junior, she led UNI to a fifth-place national finish, which included her 13th-place individual performance. A native of Dubuque, she is also a member of the Dubuque Senior High School Athletic Hall of Fame.

How can parents most effectively support their child(ren) as a junior athlete(s)?

What if we simply asked this question without the word effectively? Does that change the question? Does it get simpler or harder to answer?

The first answer to this question for me would be, do what they can. My parents didn't have a lot of money, so what I got from them was probably a lot different than other kids playing golf. Neither is better or worse, they're just different. Parents shouldn't focus on those differences, but instead do the best they can. Here's how my parents did that for me.

1. My parents made me invest in myself. If I wanted new clubs or new shoes, I had to pay half. I worked from age 14 on and while I wasn't much of a saver, I did understand goals. When I wanted those Hogan Apex irons, I started saving for them so I could pay my half. It made me value my equipment and my paychecks.

2. My parents gave me opportunities. They couldn't leave town for multi-day tournaments, but they could find a trusted competitor who would take me along. They found ways to get me where I needed to go most of the time, and it allowed me to spend time with older players with whom I wouldn't normally hang out.

3. My parents were pushy in a sneaky way. If I was sitting around on a sunny day, they'd ask me if I'd like to clean out the garage or work on my putting. In other words, they didn't want to see me sitting around, but they still somehow made practice seem like a good option and my choice.

4. My parents never treated me like my score. They were happy for me, not with me, when I played well. They were disappointed for me, not in me, when I had rough days. Our supper table was rarely about my results, but often about who I played with, how her mom was doing, who else I saw and what was fun about the day. For my family, sports were about relationships and stories.

If my parents were worried about being effective, I'm not sure the support they offered me would look quite the same. They really just offered me love. That is what effective support should feel like.

I didn't start playing tournament golf until my freshman year in high school. I won the conference championship my senior year and got some scholarship money to play at Northern Iowa. It was a pretty short learning curve, but I know that my parents' ability to allow it to be my thing and not theirs made a difference to the time I invested and the path that I followed. I am still absolutely in love with the game.

What is one piece of advice you have for a junior athlete?

You will always be the best expert on you. Others will offer advice but weigh it against your own experience or feel for the game.

Mark said: I hope you are as blown away right now as Britt and I were in getting to meet and talk to these amazing people as we collected their guidance. One additional resource I came across recently is the book by Craig Kessler titled *The Dad Advice Project: Words of Wisdom From Guys Who Love Being Dads* - the collection of men is wildly diverse - CEOs, sales leaders, professional athletes, fathers of professional athletes, investors, lawyers, entrepreneurs, coaches ... and the one thing they all have in common is that they are dads, and they share their best advice with the rest of us.

Of particular interest to me and perhaps, most befitting the audience of the book you have in your hands is the advice of Shawn Spieth, father to Jordan and his two siblings. Shawn's advice, in part, is provided below:

Five Simple Learnings for Dads

1. *It's about Them, not Us. Teach, encourage, and enable your boys. Be sure to let them fail and grow in ways that are best for their growth. It's hard, but we need to resist the temptation to 'make' them successful.*
2. *KISS. Keep it simple and to the point. First of all, it is much easier, and second, boys usually react better to simple and to-the-point advice, feedback, and encouragement.*

3. *Answer their Questions with Questions.* *Most advice is situational, and in turn, I have found there to be very few stock, generic answers for boys. In turn, the most effective approach for me has been to answer their questions with additional leading questions until they come up with the right answer for themselves. Similar to an effective business leader or courtroom attorney.*

4. *Be a Father, not a BFF.* *We all want to be our boys' best friend, but this is a dangerous road to travel for most of us. Best case, we become one of our son's top "advisors" while also being a strong, appropriate father figure who is not afraid to use tough love where appropriate. Unfortunately, dads often fail to employ tough love in an effort to avoid conflict or to be cool. This approach usually does not end well. Your boys should have their own best friends, separate from you. That said, we can have just as much fun with them, and they will still only have one dad!*

5. *Sports.* *Sports provided an amazing opportunity for our boys to develop leadership and team skills at an early age and to continue to grow those skillsets all the way into adulthood. Preschool "athletes" have varying levels of physical and people skills they can see and develop on their own at an early age with peer and coach guidance. This happens for most children without direct parent involvement, which is awesome, and helps kids get a heads start in preparation for school and life in general.*

And another that resonated with me from the same book is Rex Kurzius, founder of Asset Panda who shared 'We are here to help shape our kids' philosophy in life and help them understand what is important. In my case, I feel like developing a work ethic, a moral compass, and ambition are examples of important concepts. It's the way our kids view the world that is important, not the latest pointer on hitting a golf ball.'

Above references excerpted from **The Dad Advice Project: Words of Wisdom From Guys Who Love Being Dads** by Craig Kessler. (c) 2021 Published by Post Hill Press.

Our hope is this section of the book becomes a living resource for you as a parent and/or junior athlete - refer back to this over and over and take the amazing advice to heart and use it to make the journey truly amazing. It is interesting given the vast array of backgrounds and journeys of the respondents there is such a strong thread of common themes. These folks have 'been there and done that', and we are humbled to be able to share their collective wisdom. We invite you to leverage the resources and contacts that have been shared above to continue to equip yourselves as parents and athletes.

What the Kids Say

When you do speak with your child be sincere - they can smell a rat and spot fake-speak, and they don't want to be patronized any more than we do.

Mark said: The irony is not lost on me that we put perhaps the most important and hard hitting chapter at the end - it's similar to why grocery stores put milk and bread in the back of the store - because they want you to walk through all that other 'stuff' on your way back there even though so many people just come in for milk and bread (if you've never thought about that, go read about it - it's a straight up marketing strategy to get us to buy something else before we make it to the register). But I digress. We felt like it was important for us to take this journey through the prior chapters to really give some meat, some context to the overall relationship that we share with our kid(s) and how hard it can be to self-reflect as a golf/sports parent - but how critical it is that we do so. Contained in the following pages are the results of an anonymous, informal survey that was shared with junior golfers to get a glimpse into their minds and hear their voices - to let them know that we are listening and striving to do our best to support them even if we do not always get it right. I find it a bit odd in writing this now, that I have always had the thought 'I am the dad, surely I know what my son needs more than he does.' Sometimes the easiest thing we can do is ask the question - kids are real, kids are honest, and kids appreciate being heard.

A sobering aside to this project - days after we solicited feedback from the junior golf community for this survey, I was at a tournament with 'Joe' from the Dollar General Cooler story above. I saw him before the start of round two, and he joked with me that I would not have wanted to see him the previous day because his son had struggled. And then he shared, 'Nah, I am just kidding ... and the reason I say that is that I had the opportunity a few nights ago to take a look at a survey (my son) was doing about his feedback on golf parents - and we had the chance to get real honest about my role and how I act and react on the golf course. I can tell you it was a hard look in the mirror at myself, and it honestly changed the way I approached this entire tournament as a dad.'

These are real, genuine, honest answers given by our kids - yours and mine - and I think we'd do well to listen to what they say - I know I will.

Britt said: Most parents don't understand why their children don't talk to them. Having a background in education, I learned early in order to get children to talk you must ask them questions that require more than a one word answer. If we really want to know what our children think, we have to be creative in how we ask them questions. Mark's question to Ben might be 'Do you want me to stay back?' which means he will stay back and watch him hit a shot and not be in the landing zone. Children usually answer yes to these types of questions because they think it is the answer their parents want them to say. No child really enjoys telling their parents no. My question to Ben would be 'Do you like it better when I stay back and watch you hit or would you prefer me to go ahead and spot the ball?' In all honesty, it really doesn't matter where I am, but I am giving Ben control over something and we all like that! It varies through the round where I stand and what I do, but I often just motion to him during a round to see what he prefers on the hole. I've learned my body language isn't always the best when he starts struggling, so I prefer to stay ahead when that is happening.

Usually, after a few holes, he will motion for me to come back because he wants something to eat! That could be true, but I also think he likes someone with him to listen to the mumbling and complaining. I'm torn between allowing mumbling and complaining and not. First of all, no one wants to hear it and it makes me uncomfortable to see someone talking to himself - even though I do it all the time. Secondly, I feel like it doesn't allow anyone to move on from the mistake or the error because it's still on topic. If anyone walks beside me they will often hear me clear my throat. That's my signal to cut it out and be quiet. I can't help but let him mumble a little, but I think children need redirection or they will continue to go down a woe is me path.

The reason I'm torn in these situations goes back to what Mark mentioned in the Carrot and the Stick section about the day Ben was mumbling to himself on the course, and we thought he was griping and complaining but told us later he was praying for strength to reset. I'll never argue with him about praying. I listen now to what he is saying and try to do my best to be positive and encourage him when he is heading down a path of getting in a funk.

Regarding the survey below and how you could use something like this - similar questions and such with your own child, I would say be creative in how questions are asked to children, don't get hurt feelings if they don't want to talk to you and give them their space to cool off if needed. Addressing these things at home when everyone is out of the pressure of the game is best. If you feel like you are losing control and need to speak to your child, walk away and look at the birds, look for lost golf balls, or even do like Ben and pray walking up the fairway.

Junior Golf: How Can Parents Best Support You, The Golfer?

(Anonymous Survey, Spring 2021)

What one word describes your parent(s)' support of your junior golf?

(Most frequently occurring answers provided)

- Energetic
- Unconditional
- Encouraging
- Committed
- Amazing
- Patient
- Awesome
- Consistent
- Understanding
- Always proud
- Supportive
- Sacrifices
- Helpful

I enjoy it when my parent(s) come to watch me play golf:

Agree - 66.7%

Disagree - 3.7%

Neutral - 29.6%

What do you like MOST about your parents watching you play golf?

(Most frequently occurring answers provided)

- Photos
- I feel that I have people there who are fully in support of me and believe in me
- Always keep me going, help me when I have a bad hole/shot
- Food and drink
- Giving me supportive and uplifting words
- Support, encouragement and watching my success and failure
- The motivation
- Encouraging me while playing
- I like when they cheer me on and supply me with food and drink
- When I hit a good shot and they are impressed
- To be able to talk about that great shot you hit so many years later
- I feel supported and cheered on
- I like being able to show out and make them proud
- Know they care
- They get excited when I play well
- When it's comfortable to have a familiar face

What do you like LEAST about your parents watching you play golf?

(Most frequently occurring answers provided)

- Pressure
- The pressure of not wanting to disappoint them
- Nerves
- Disagreement of decision making

- Makes it more stressful
- When they criticize me
- Sometimes get too involved and try to help too much when I don't need it
- One was an accomplished player so it was hard to do some things on my own without attention
- When I was younger they used to be hard on me, before I told them how much added pressure that put on me. After that they weren't hard on me and only supportive!
- When they tell me to keep my head up and things like that because when I'm mad I just want to be left alone.
- They put a bit of pressure on me (mainly mental for me)
- Sometimes on my worst days it gets hard to control myself mentally especially when they are present because temper is a big thing with them and I've always struggled mentally
- The reaction after a bad shot or bad round
- Being frustrated when I play bad
- The nerves
- Feeling like I'm disappointing them
- They don't want to because it creates too much pressure
- They make me nervous and I feel like I need to play well

Why do you play competitive junior golf? (Select all that apply)

I love the game - 88.9%

I love to compete - 85.2%

As a way to help me pay for college - 29.6%

To please my parents - 11.1%

Additional write-in responses:

I want to play golf at high collegiate and professional level - 3.7%

Golf Benefits you no matter what path you take in life - 3.7%

When I am upset on the golf course, the best thing my parent(s) can say to me or do for me is:

(Most frequently occurring answers provided)

- Get me some food
- Encourage me to let it go and focus on what is in front of me
- Don't talk to me
- Settle down/Stay Patient
- Just to have fun
- Leave me alone
- Tell me to get it back on the next holes
- Tell me to keep going and don't regret the things that I've already done
- Let it go; by the time you get the next tee it's over
- We'll still let you eat dinner tonight. Life goes on.
- Hug me
- Just smile and give me a fist bump or something like that, keep it simple
- Don't say anything - just ignore me.
- Nothing let me figure it out
- Leave me alone
- Keep grinding
- Just be quiet or say it's ok
- Tell me to calm down
- Just to have fun
- Just smile and say shake it off
- I know you tried your hardest

What is one thing you wish your parent(s) would STOP doing at your tournaments?

(Most frequently occurring answers provided)

- Forgetting to silence phones
- Talking to me too much
- Giving a pep talk when I don't necessarily need one
- Telling me things that I already know
- Getting too involved and start giving me swing tips or pointers in the middle of my round
- Shaking their head in disapproval
- Sometimes they would shake their head when they thought I wasn't looking
- Trying to encourage me when I'm doing bad
- Being so into it that I feel pressured to do well
- Stop being as uptight whenever I hit a bad shot or drop a club after swinging. I could be doing a lot worse.
- Putting pressure on me to play well
- Being frustrated when I play bad
- Acting like they might know everything
- I wish my dad would stop shaking his head when I mess up
- Talking too much
- My parents don't watch but other parents have too many opinions. Let us figure it out.
- When I hit a bad shot stop pacing around
- Being frustrated when I play bad

What is one thing you wish your parent(s) would START doing at your tournaments?

(Most frequently occurring answers provided)

- Taking more photos
- Being relaxed whenever things go bad
- Keeping my stats
- Marking down things about my swing/round etc and tell me about it after the round
- Interacting with me a little more in between holes
- Trying to be better about how they speak to me after
- I wish they would take some more pictures and videos so I can break down what I was doing well and doing poorly
- Just be ok with if I play golf or not
- Being more quiet and be more off in the distance
- My parents don't watch per my request
- Stay positive during the tournament

What is one thing you wish your parent(s) would KEEP doing at your tournaments?

(Most frequently occurring answers provided)

- Motivating me
- Stay behind me and don't let me see them too much
- Positivity and words of encouragement
- Giving me drinks/snacks
- Always be there
- Keep coming to them
- Encouraging me
- Showing their support through cheering
- Usually having limited conversation with me and leaving me to my own thoughts

- Keep supporting me
- Keep giving me confidence boosts when I hit a good shot. They are always the main people I hear.
- Helping look for balls and being engaged
- Coming to tournaments
- Showing up on the back nine to just watch nine holes

I think my parent(s) want me to succeed more than I want me to succeed

>Agree - 22.2%
>
>Disagree - 37%
>
>Neutral - 40.7%

I feel like the mood of my parent(s) is dependent upon how I play (i.e., if I play well, everyone is happy - if I play poorly, everyone is mad)

>Agree - 22.2%
>
>Disagree - 51.9%
>
>Neutral - 25.9%

I believe my parents when they say that "It doesn't matter how you play today as long as you do your best"

>Agree - 51.9%
>
>Disagree - 48.1%

I feel like my parents love me less if I play poorly:

Agree - 11.1%
Disagree - 88.9%
Neutral - 0%

I think I would enjoy my round more and play better if my parent(s) was/were not there:

Agree - 18.5%
Disagree - 59.3%
Neutral - 22.2%

Golf is still fun to play, and I enjoy it

Agree - 100%

I would give up playing competitive golf if I thought it would not disappoint my parent(s).

Yes - 3.7%
No - 85.2%
Maybe - 11.1%

In a short sentence, what is the best way for your parents to support you as a golfer?

(Highlighted responses below)

- Always be behind you whether you play well or not on any given day
- Keep encouraging me, don't try and get too involved while I'm playing, let me do my own thing and we can talk after the match.

- I play better when I can focus on golf and have no one watching me
- Give me words of encouragement on and off the course
- Understand that this is the hardest game in the world and support the ups and downs because they are going to happen.
- Love us regardless, be there throughout the whole process not just tournaments if we play good, be consistently supportive
- A parent should always be understanding that golf is not a game of perfect
- Congratulate me when I play good, tell me what to work on and improve upon no matter if I play good or bad. Take me to the course when I want to go and help pay for equipment and tournaments.
- Be there for me and let me have my highs and lows, let me figure out how to fix things and not try to fix them themselves
- Just being supportive and helping along the journey be ok with the bad rounds
- To be supportive and to not be angry when I play bad as long as I did my best they should not be angry
- Help and to be there every step of the way
- To show up and remain in a good mood
- Stop trying to give advice, we have coaches who do that
- Paying for golf lessons and clubs to help enhance my skills

What Ben Says

'No legacy is so rich as honesty.'

—WILLIAM SHAKESPEARE

The game of golf is supposed to be relaxing and fun. One thing to always remember is enjoy every moment of each round because you won't relive those moments again. It sucks to play bad and have things not go your way but that is what golf is. It's about who can respond better to the adversity because everyone will have adversity of some type throughout the round.

I started playing golf competitively at a young age and could see my potential but it never would click out on the golf course. I thought it was my game that was struggling when I went out and played in a tournament. I met with a mental/confidence coach (coach Tami that my parents mentioned) and realized that the only thing that holds you back on the golf course is a negative attitude. Your mind will do what you put into it - if you get over a shot and think 'don't go left', you are most likely going to hit it left. After meeting with the coach Tami my thoughts changed from 'don't go left' to 'I will hit this shot down the right side'. I personally think having a great attitude and positive thinking will shave many shots off of the scorecard. This doesn't mean you can't get mad when you hit a bad shot, you just can't get over the next shot mad and let it affect you there. If you have a good attitude and positive thoughts while you play a round it will be super easy to enjoy the moment.

Playing bad isn't the end of the world either. As I got older I began to realize that the day after you play bad no one gives a hoot about it. The most important part of the game is the short game. It took me a while to realize that the short game is where 'the money is made'. If you can't get up and down then you will not score well. Chipping and putting should be at least 85% of your practice time.

Parents are a big part of the game of golf but can also be a big barrier. Parents can help with the mental aspect of the child's game by giving them encouragement and helping with swing tips. Parents can hurt the kids if they become too serious. It is all about enjoying the game for the child as they continue to get better. You can't force the kid to play well, it has to come naturally.

Some kids bloom at different times of their junior golf career. For me personally, I think the game started to click a little later than all of the kids I was playing with. It is a big thing to make sure your kids don't get intimidated by the kids that have bloomed early. I know some kids that let that affect their way of playing the game. For example, kids would start changing the patient way of playing into the, no good, aggressive mentality. It is important to teach your children that the game will come when it comes and the hard work they put in will pay off.

I am a firm believer that you get out what you put in. If you practice once a week then that is the result you will get when you take it to competition, but if you are practicing for 5 days a week you will get the result of that when playing in a tournament. Practicing needs to be taken seriously without taking out the fun. Incorporating fun little games into your child's practice time is necessary in order to keep their interest in the game. I've always loved playing golf and a big reason for that is because my dad and my coaches instilled fun games into my practice time. The big thing for parents is keeping the game fun while being serious so that your kids are enjoying the process of getting better.

God blessed me with some pretty great golf parents. The kind that yells a little, loves a little, and gets mad a little bit more, but then always ends up loving me in the end. My parents love me no matter how I play and that is a big part of why I am still playing golf today. They get mad and yell at me because of my horrible attitude at times but at the end they always add 'I love you'.

I love my parents watching me play and every time I walk off the 18th green I hear 'I'm proud of you', and that means the most. It helps with the love of the game when my parents are always encouraging me throughout the round. They could care less if I play badly and it took me a while to understand that part of it. They only care about me having fun and not having a bad attitude because that is the worst thing you could have when walking the golf course.

My mom is the encourager and is always telling me 'you've got this.' She can sneak some snacks into my hand too, and that always makes the round a little bit better. My dad is a realist, every time I try to make an excuse or complain he tells me that it is part of golf, and everyone is dealing with the same conditions. I think it has made me a better golfer to have both of them feeding into me as I get better and enjoy the cool little game called golf.

My answers to the two questions asked in the **Advice from People Who Know** section are below:

How can parents most effectively support their child(ren) as a junior athlete(s)? Parents can most effectively support their child by always encouraging them to continue to do what they love. Parents don't need to push their child to play a sport that they aren't enjoying. Also parents need to always make sure that the game is fun for their child. Parents need to remember that kids are kids and they are going to get mad at times when playing badly, and it will take a little bit of maturing for them to realize that attitude has the biggest effect on the game.

What is one piece of advice you have for a junior athlete? The biggest thing is to always have a good attitude. I know it is hard because I struggled with it, too. But having a good attitude makes the game a lot easier and more enjoyable and when you enjoy what you are doing, you will play better.

Always have fun and enjoy what you are doing. If you have buddies that play the same sports as you, practice with them and challenge each other and you will become a better player. One of the best ways to become better is by playing against people that are better than you.

Recommended Resources

BOOKS

- The Confident Athlete by Tami Matheny
- Looking for a FULL RIDE? by Renee Lopez
- The Dad Advice Project: Words of Wisdom From Guys Who Love Being Dads by Craig Kessler
- Parentshift by Hernan Chousa
- This is Good - A Journey of Overcoming Adversity by Tami Matheny
- Golf from Point A by Susie Meyers
- Golf is Not a Game of Perfect by Dr. Bob Rotella
- Every Shot Counts by Mark Broadie
- Harvey Penick's Little Red Book: Lessons And Teachings From A Lifetime In Golf by Harvey Penick

FACEBOOK GROUPS

- This is Good
- Reformed Sports Project
- Parents and the Mental Game
- Operation 36 Golf Program
- Looking for a FULL RIDE?
- Educating Parents of HS Athletes on The College Recruiting Process
- The Drive Home: The Youth Athlete/Parent Dynamic
- ILoveToWatchYouPlay

Contact the Authors

BrittandMarkTheDriveHome@gmail.com

Connect with Refuse2LoseCoaching
(Tami Matheny)
Website: http://r2lc.com/
Email: TamiLMatheny@gmail.com

Pity Party Performance Level (3PL)

This is a self-created resource (by Mark) leveraging tools from trusted advisors. The concept may seem completely off the wall so please use only as you deem appropriate. This is offered as a practical tool to use if you feel it is relevant to your situation. I am by no means a sports psychologist and don't even play one on TV - but I think in pictures, and hope that this image can be helpful. I realize the graphic will not win any awards - but you get the point.

Our Focus Tanks: Are We Robbing Our Performance? I Think So.

Mark McKinney, 2021

When we approach a task – work, sports, family, etc. – we have X amount of brain capacity to focus on that task. With so many things going on in our daily lives … our brains compartmentalize enough capacity for us to be successful on that 'thing' – it's just how we are wired.

The BUT, though, is that we have to help our brains by letting them do what they are designed to do … and by not getting in the way of it and well, screwing it up.

What I mean is this … use playing basketball as an example. Say we have a big game that we are playing in … our brains set aside ENOUGH space in there to deal with just that game … it already filters out all the other junk in our day … girlfriend, work, tests, money, whatever – so the game gets its own special allotment of focus.

That space, though, that is set aside for the focus on the game only works well if we let it operate on the absolute present moment … and the task/decision/play in front of us. If we try to steal any amount of that space to use for focusing on 'what might' happen in the 4th quarter … OR, what happened to us 6 minutes ago … our brains are not as efficient.

Think about it in a numerical sense … we have already said that our brain sets aside the specific space to focus on this game … so in that space, there is **100% available focus** space for the game. Meaning that, in the moment … if I use it correctly, I always have 100% available to me – and if I use that 100% … I am as good as I can be – I can operate at my absolute best. I cannot control bad bounces, others' actions, if a shot goes in or misses, etc. … but if I use that 100% … I will do MY absolute best in that moment.

Picture this: 5 minutes into the game you get a foul called on you that is an absolute garbage call … ref missed it – and you are upset about it – which is fine, in that moment. You use your 100% focus to process it

… and ideally, move on from it. But what if you don't let it go … what if you still hold that call in the back of your mind … 3 minutes, 10 minutes, 20 minutes later and say, it is taking up 25% of your available focus space. Guess what … that 100% we were working with earlier … is now at 75%.

Based on that one bad call that went against you which we CANNOT go back and change … by allowing ANY of our thoughts to remain there … you have robbed your present and future performance by 25%. Are we as good at 75% as we are at 100%? Absolutely not. Can we do anything to change what has happened in the past? Absolutely not. We have heard it said – 'don't let that one call get you twice' meaning … don't let that one call, which you thought was bad, lead you to making

> **'Your double bogey hasn't ruined your scorecard. Your inability to forget it has'**
>
> *@MeAndMyGolf on Instagram*

another poor decision and either getting another foul called, making a bad pass, etc. Sit back and watch athletes who cannot let go of things … It's like clockwork to watch that one call **get 'em twice**.

Now, think about it in a golfing context. Each shot is deserving of our 100% focus … and our brains have set aside that focus space just as discussed above. We get into the round and get a strange bounce or hit a bad shot that leads to a double bogey. We have two choices (1) give 100% of our focus in that moment to understanding what happened … accept it and move forward giving our next moment the available 100% … or (2) we leave 25% … 30% … 10% of our mind stewing over the fact that we made a double bogey … and we ROB our next shot, our next moment of all of the available focus capacity. In #2, I stand over my next tee shot … say at 75% …. which in turn may lead to a bad swing … and guess what … 'it got me twice'.

It is as clear as day to external observers the athletes that can let a bad hole/play go and return to their 100% on the very next moment. It is even more clear, the athletes that can't. Their minds race, they are upset and mad at themselves because of what 'could have been' … and they rob their area of focus … and it begins. Operating for the next X minutes or X holes at less than 100% … UNTIL such a point that it finally washes over them, and they realize that they have let that one thing, that thing in the past that they cannot control … control their focus.

That time … that time between the 'something bad' happening and getting back to 100% focus – let's call it 3PL … Pity Party Performance Level. Meaning that … I have allowed my level of focus to drop below 100% … while I have my pity party. The sooner you bounce back from 3PL to 100%, the sooner you are back at peak performance.

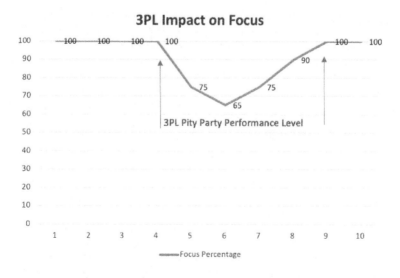

Some never bounce back in a round/game ... and their focus level falls even lower - the truly mentally strong **bounce back immediately**.

And that, simply put, is the clear, unmistakable line of separation between your best on a given day versus something less than your capabilities. Protect your 100% from theft ... and you can do it because you are the only one that can steal from it. You control it ... YOU control it. YOU CONTROL it. YOU CONTROL IT.

So, what's your focus tank look like ... in the moment? Check yourself throughout your round/game. Ask yourself ... visualize the tank ... and keep it full.

Strategies for Minimizing/Eliminating 3PL:

Taken directly from the 'Stay in The Moment' chapter of Tami Matheny's book This is Good the strategies below are game changers ... literally!

...However, we can train our brains to stay in the moment through various exercises and tips. Below you will find several suggestions (by no means is this an exhaustive list):

<Document author's note: Pick ONE of the below and implement it for your next tournament/game situation. You'll go nuts trying to do them all ... keep it simple, find one that feels right and roll with it.>

1. ***Deep Breathing:*** *Breathing is simple and something we already do, but we also take it for granted and don't pay attention to it. Setting aside time to do some focused breathing or meditation will train our brain to be able to take that one deep breath on cue.*

Another great exercise to increase focus is to breathe in for seven counts. As you breathe in, breathing in positive emotions. As you breathe out, see the negative emotions leaving your body.

2. **Use your five senses:** *Taste, touch, smell, see, hear. Being fully immersed in a sense helps you stay in the moment. For instance, focusing intently on what you are hearing keeps you in the present moment. The key is to get fully immersed in that sense.*

3. **Stare at the sky for 10 seconds:** *This movement breaks the emotion you are having. When you bring your eyes back immediately have a positive thought or emotion to now focus on.*

4. **Close your eyes:** *When we do this simple action, it activates parts of our brain linked to our imagination and multi-sensory activity. It helps us focus. It is why we often close our eyes when we are trying to remember an important name or detail.*

5. **Use the acronym W.I.N:** *"What's Important Now?". Asking yourself this question can often refocus your mind back to what you need to do at that moment. When we win the moment, we move to the next one.*

6. **Use a mantra:** *"First things first" is a good mantra. Often, we allow our brains to get overwhelmed by the big picture. Similar to W.I.N., we are breaking down our focus to one thing. What's the first thing you need to do? Do it and then allow yourself to think about the next thing and so on. Another good one to repeat is "Right Here, Right Now." Or use a mantra that will remind you to get back to this moment, this play or this breath! The key to success is to stay focused on what's important in that moment. Learning to win the moment will change your life.*

Afterword

Mark and Britt have shared their own experiences of their local and primarily state junior golf journey with their son, Ben, though their advice can certainly extend to a junior golf experience on a larger level. Many parents are unaware of the effects their actions and reactions have on their children as they participate in youth sports, and in particular for this book, golf. All children are different, as are all youth athletes, but all readers can find a behavior or strategy to implement or change regarding their interactions before, during, or after a youth golf tournament. A fellow golf parent often says, "Golf is hard." We don't need to make the game of golf any harder for our children than it already is.

I enjoyed reliving the stories in print Mark and Britt included and noting the lessons they learned along the way, but I most value the input provided by the junior golfers in **What the Kids Say**. Again, all children are different. One of mine looks at me disapprovingly when I have my phone out taking pictures during a round and the other wants to see the pictures I took after a round. The input provided allows you to have a conversation with your child about his/her preferences regarding your behavior as a parent as you watch or don't watch the round.

The **Advice from People Who Know** section allows the reader to see through the lenses of people who have witnessed both positive and negative impacts parents have on youth athletes over time. Some of them have been observers, while others have seen direct effects regarding their own children and their parenting behavior and decisions.

Most of us strive to better ourselves, and most of us will also admit that we don't always get "this parenting thing" right. Learning from both the mistakes and advice from others can help us have more enjoyable drives home.

— Staci Howard, Golf Mom & Villager

Made in the USA
Monee, IL
29 April 2022